Point Reyes National Seashore

A Hiking and Nature Guide

Don and Kay Martin
Illustrated by Bob Johnson

Inquiries should be addressed to:
Martin Press
P.O. Box 2109
San Anselmo, CA 94979

ISBN 0-9617044-6-2

Printed in the United States of America

Cover Photo © 1991 Ed Cooper

Barbara Koeth

Acknowledgments

We are extremely grateful to all of those who have helped and encouraged us in writing both the first and second editions of this book. At the National Park Service, we thank John Del`Osso, Jack Williams, Carlin Finke, Loretta Farley, Don Neubacher, Sarah Allen, Bill Michaels and especially Dewey Livingston, who provided valuable historical information and reviewed parts of the original manuscript.

A special thanks to those we consulted for natural history information, Geoff Geupel at PRBO, Jim Locke, Al Molina and Joe Mueller at the College of Marin. We are also grateful to Sue Baty from the Jack Mason Museum who provided historical photos. Thanks also to Tom Gaman for providing data for making the maps and to Tom Harrison, whose trail map we used to get improved mileage data.

We would also like to thank our hiking and running friends who have shared many enjoyable times on the trails of Marin with us: Dick and Sharon Shlegeris, Bill and Dixie James, Ruth and Steve Nash, Shel and Joy Siewert, Arlene Hansen, Mary Lou Grossberg, Sue Steele, Mel and Pam DeWeerd, Dave and Rozanne Stringer, Jim and Joanne Kambur, Bill and Els Tuinzing, Edda Stickle and Gillian Clark. We especially want to thank the members of our family, Daryl Odnert and Jennifer, Theresa, Susan and Greg Martin, for their enthusiastic and valuable support.

Picture Credits
14 - Bear Valley Country Club: Anne T. Kent California Room, Marin
        County Library
60 - Schooner *Point Reyes:* Point Reyes National Seashore
70 - Tule Elk: photo by John Aho, Point Reyes National Seashore
72 - The Oaks: Jack Mason Museum
93 - Lighthouse: Dewey Livingston, Point Reyes National Seashore
94 - Elephant Seal: Dr. Sally Fairfax
95 - California Sea Lion: Dr. Sally Fairfax
118 - Golden Hind watercolor: artist William Gilkerson, courtesy of
        National Maritime Museum, SF National Maritime Historic Park
120 - Wreck of the *Samoa:* photo by Mrs. Clarence R. Pape, courtesy
        National Maritime Museum, SF National Maritime Historic Park
120 - Home Ranch: Jack Mason Museum
All other photos are by the authors.

Table of Contents

How to Use This Book
Most Frequently Asked Questions

About Point Reyes

Point Reyes National Seashore was established by President John F. Kennedy on September 13, 1962. Today, the park consists of 75,000 acres with about one-third of the land leased to dairy ranches. This pastoral zone lies in the western section of the park where the land is flatter and mostly grassland.

Another one-third of the park has been declared the Philip Burton Wilderness Area where man-made structures and vehicles are not allowed. This area lies mostly along the forested western slopes of Inverness Ridge and along the ocean beaches.

The remaining third of the park is more developed with various park buildings, roads and bicycle trails.

Point Reyes is open daily from sunrise to sunset throughout the year. The main Visitor Center, located at Bear Valley, is open weekdays, 9am to 5pm, weekends and holidays 8am to 5pm. Maps and information are available, as well as restrooms and a picnic area. A list of free naturalist activities is published in the quarterly visitors guide. Phone 415-663-1092 for information.

Bear Valley Visitor Center

The best way to get to the Visitor Center from Hwy. 101 is to take the Sir Francis Drake turnoff in Greenbrae and go west through San Anselmo and Fairfax all the way to Olema. At Hwy 1, go right for 200 yds then left on Bear Valley Rd. for the last half mile. This route is 23 miles long, but the driving time is forty-five minutes to an hour depending on traffic.

Over two million people come to Point Reyes each year. Most of them concentrate in the areas of Bear Valley, Drakes Beach, Limantour Beach and the Point Reyes Headlands, consisting of Chimney Rock and the Point Reyes Lighthouse. While these magnificent areas deserve their popularity, we hope you will use this book to get out and explore *all* of Point Reyes.

Happy Hiking!

How to Use This Book

Choosing A Hike or Outing

When planning a hike or outing, the first consideration should be the weather. For example, in summer, the coast is often cold and foggy, especially in the morning. The fog usually clears off by noon, then returns with strong northwest winds in the late afternoon.

Two other factors to consider when choosing a hike are distance and elevation change. If you are new to Point Reyes or new to hiking, it's best to choose a hike conservatively. Three miles of hiking in mountainous terrain can take twice as long and be twice as hard as three miles on flat terrain.

Once you've selected a range of distances and elevations, there are several questions you might consider. What is the best hike for this season? What wildflowers are in bloom? Where are the best view hikes? The best hikes in hot weather? A good place to begin answering these questions is to look at the suggested hikes in Appendix A1 and A2.

Hike Descriptions

Here is a sample entry of a hike description with a brief explanation.

> *Distance:* 6.9 miles   Shaded: 60%
> *Elevation Change:* 1300'   Occasionally steep.
> *Rating:* Hiking - 10   Some poison oak.
> *When to Go:* Excellent anytime, best from March to June.

Distance and Shade

Distance measurements refer to the **total** hike distance. Shaded refers to the percent of tree cover. Shaded 60% means that the total distance is shaded about 60% by trees or tall shrubs.

Elevation Change

Elevation Change helps determine how strenuous the hike is. A 1300' change means the hike climbs 1300' and descends 1300'.

Hiking Rating

The Hiking Rating depends on aesthetics. How interesting is the hike? For example, the Bear Valley-Old Pine-Sky trails, Hike F3, has a variety of flora, rolling terrain and good views. We consider it interesting 90-100% of the time and so, rated it a 10.

1

Hiking Rating

8	Interesting 70-80% of the time
9	Interesting 80-90% of the time
10	Interesting 90-100% of the time

Obviously, this rating system is subjective and depends on what we like. Also, our rating of hikes is based on the best possible conditions, the best season, views, weather and wildflowers.

When To Go

The When To Go rating is based on flora and fauna, weather, season, views, trail and road conditions. Winter provides rainfall and water runoff. Late winter and spring produce wildflowers. Fall often has the best weather. These seasons are the best times to go on most hikes.

Using The Maps

The lower 3-dimensional map contains "3-D slices" as shown in the figure below. The bottom map is displayed so that no part of the map is any closer to the observer than any other part. Scales shown on the map are approximate since elevations have been exaggerated.

View of a 3-D map slice.

Behind slice it is empty and black.

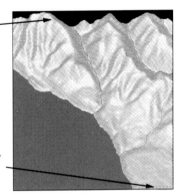

Front of slice is grey with vertical stripes to show elevation changes.

Symbols used on the maps.

- - - - - - - - - -	Hikers Only
- - - -»»- - - -	Very Steep - Arrow Points Uphill
— — — — —	Bicycles Allowed
——————	Roads and Cars
🏠	Ranger Station or Visitor Center
🚶	Trailhead
🚐	Pickup Cars for Shuttle Hike
❶	Junction Number

Suggestions and Precautions

As hiking becomes more popular, it attracts a wider variety of people with different levels of hiking experience. We offer the following suggestions and precautions, especially for beginning hikers.

What to Take on a Hike

The three most essential items to take on hikes are a map, fluids and clothes for protection from fog or wind. However, when hiking in more remote areas on Point Reyes, it is best to be prepared. Here is a sample check list of things to take.

Adequate Fluids	First Aid Kit
Light Jacket	Extra Food
Poncho in Winter	Hat
Sunscreen in Summer	Whistle
Guide Book or Map	Flashlight
Binoculars	Compass
Knife	

Hiking Boots

Most of the trails described in this book are uneven, rocky or rutted. Hiking boots are preferred. They protect the feet and provide stable support. They reduce the chance of injuries, such as sprained ankles.

Hiking Alone

Hiking alone is not recommended. However, if you do go out alone, tell someone where you are going and when you will return or leave a note in your car at the trailhead with this information.

Fluids

Fluids are essential when hiking or staying outdoors. Often, people go hiking or go to the beach and end the day with a mild headache. Usually, this is attributed to too much exposure, too much sun or too much wind. Many times, the problem is too little fluids. Hiking requires a minimum of 1/2 quart of fluid per hour, or more, depending on the temperature and elevation change.

Plan to drink at least 1/2 quart of fluid per hour on hikes.

Alcohol does not count. It is a diuretic, which means that it removes fluid by osmosis in the stomach. It is always a good idea to carry water on a hike and to drink it regularly whether you feel thirsty or not.

Do not drink water from streams or lakes. It may contain giardia, which can cause severe stomach problems until medically treated.

3

Hikers and Bicyclists

Hikes in this book have been laid out to minimize contact between hikers and bicyclists. Where possible, hikes have been routed off bike roads and onto trails. Also, hikes that include roads for part of the trip usually head uphill, so that hikers can see bicyclists coming downhill. All bike roads are marked on the maps.

Poison Oak

Poison oak for some is a minor irritation, for most, a major irritation and for a few, a medical emergency. The best advice is to learn to identify the plant by its leaves and avoid touching it. An old saying is,

"Leaves of three, leave it be."

In fall, poison oak leaves turn crimson red and drop off. In winter, the bare branches are difficult to identify, yet still retain their toxic oils. It helps to stay on designated   trails and to watch out for

Poison Oak

branches that lean out onto the trail. If you are allergic to it, carry small individually packaged Handi-wipes and wash an affected area within ten minutes.

Ticks and Lyme Disease

Ticks are common at Point Reyes and are especially noticeable during the rainy season from November to May. Recent studies have shown that 1-2% of the western black-legged ticks in Marin County carry Lyme disease.

The best way to avoid ticks is to stay on trails. It also helps to wear light clothing so that ticks can be seen. Be sure to brush yourself frequently, especially after passing through tall grass or shrubs. After a hike, check yourself completely. Ticks anesthetize the skin before biting so you'll seldom feel the original bite.

Western Black-Legged Tick - enlarged 8 times

Early removal of a tick reduces the risk of infection. Use tweezers. Grab the tick mouth parts as close to the skin as possible and pull straight out. Wash hands and clean the bite with an antiseptic.

The first recognizable symptom of Lyme disease is usually a ring-like rash that occurs 3-30 days after the tick bite. One or more rashes may occur and not always at the bite. However, a rash only appears 60-80% of the time. Other symptoms may include flu-like fever, chills, fatigue, headaches and a stiff neck. Since early diagnosis of Lyme disease is crucial, see a doctor if you think you have it.

Identifying Birds, Flora and Fauna

Each hike includes information about the birds, wildflowers and animals that may be seen. Appendices A9 to A17 provide references to help identify them. Also, the back inside cover contains sketches of animal tracks that might be seen.

Wildflowers are identified using their common names. Sometimes, we use one common name to refer to more than one species of a flowering plant. For example, there are three species of lupine on Point Reyes, but we do not distinguish between them in the hike description. In the Appendix, we describe just one species of each kind of wildflower.

Rattlesnakes and Mountain Lions

Both are present and dangerous, but rarely seen at Point Reyes. Rattlesnakes will often sun themselves in open areas in the spring. The best way to avoid rattlesnakes is to stay on the trail and avoid climbing over loose rocky areas.

If you do see a mountain lion, don't run. Stand your ground, keep eye contact, make yourself look bigger, perhaps using your jacket or daypack. Then, slowly back away. If attacked, fight back.

Parking

Remember to lock your car and don't leave valuables in view. Vandalism and theft at trailheads is not common, but it does happen. You might check with park rangers about problem areas.

Getting Lost

It is not easy to get lost on hikes. The park service has done a good job of placing signs at trail junctions. However, if you are new to the area, our advice is to follow the book carefully and note each junction on the map. Stay on trails and don't take shortcuts.

Disclaimer

Although we have tried to provide valuable information, errors may occur. Also, nature is not static. Hillsides erode. Trees fall down. Trails get rerouted. Signs change and hikes change. In winter, some trails are impassable. This book is only a guide. *We can not accept responsibility for trail conditions or for trail information.* This is our disclaimer that we do not accept liability or legal responsibility for any injuries, damage, or losses allegedly caused by using this book. For the best information, check with the rangers at the Visitor Center at Bear Valley.

Most Frequently Asked Questions

We asked the rangers at the Bear Valley Visitor Center what questions were asked most often. Here is their list with answers.

RESOURCES

Where is the restroom located?

There are two restrooms at Bear Valley. One is located at the entrance to the Visitor Center on the right hand side just before entering the doors. The second restroom is located 200 yds. east of the Visitor Center next to the picnic area.

Where is the nearest store?

Within three miles of the Visitor Center, there are grocery stores in Olema and Inverness Park. Other stores are located in Inverness, Point Reyes Station, Stinson Beach and Bolinas. For other resources, see Appendix 22.

Are there any ranger led activities at Point Reyes?

Yes, there are a variety of naturalist hikes, talks and walks occurring on weekends throughout the year. A quarterly Visitors Guide and the Visitors Center list all activities.

WHALES

Where is the best place to see whales?

The lighthouse is the best place.

When is the best time to see whales?

The peak of southern migration occurs in the first two weeks of January. The northern migration lasts longer, peaking in the middle of March, but extending to the end of May.

How close to shore do the whales come?

Some come within 300 yds., while a half-mile or 800 yds. is common.

How long does it take to get to the lighthouse?

It's 20 miles from the Visitor Center and takes about 45 minutes.

Is it foggy there?

The lighthouse is the second foggiest location on the continent (after Nantucket) and also the windiest point on the West Coast.

It is usually foggy in summer, and less foggy during whale migration. See the Visitor Center bulletin board for current weather information.

ELEPHANT SEALS AND SEA LIONS

Where can you see these marine mammals?

Both can be seen out at the Point Reyes Headlands. Elephant seals can usually be seen at Chimney Rock from December to March. Sea Lions can be seen at the Sea Lion Overlook on the way to the Point Reyes lighthouse. See Appendix 8 for more information.

HIKING AND WILDFLOWERS

How do I get to the Earthquake trail?

The Earthquake trail starts from the northern end of the main parking lot next to the restroom. See Hike 1.

What is the best hike for newcomers to Point Reyes?

Start on the Bear Valley trail. For a 3-mile hike, go out to Divide Meadow and back. For a good 8-mile hike, go to Arch Rock at the ocean and then retrace your steps back.

Where is the best place to see wildflowers?

Chimney Rock, Abbotts Lagoon and Kehoe Beach are generally best with flowers starting in late February and peaking in April - May.

Are dogs allowed on trails? How about the beach?

Not on trails. Dogs can be taken on a leash on Limantour Beach, Point Reyes Beach North and South, and Kehoe Beach.

OCEAN AND BEACHES

What is the temperature of the ocean?

The average ocean temperature ranges from 50-57 °F.

Is there any place to swim at Point Reyes?

Some people wade at Limantour and Drakes Beach, but there is no lifeguard on duty. Swimming is possible in Tomales Bay, at Marshall Beach and at Tomales Bay State Park. The ocean beaches, Point Reyes Beach, Kehoe and McClures Beach are unsafe for wading.

Are sharks a problem at the beach?

No. However, great white sharks do inhabit the waters and can be a problem for surfers, abalone divers and kayakers.

RANCHES

Why are there cows in the park?

Legislation creating the park preserved some of the ranches that have been here for over 100 years. The park leases the land to the ranchers, about 21,000 acres or 1/3 of the park area.

1 Bear Valley Interpretive Trails

Distance: 0.6, 0.7 and 0.8 miles   Shaded: 70%
Elevation Change: No more than 150'
Rating: Hiking - 10
When to Go: Excellent anytime, best in spring.
These three interpretive trails all have information signs explaining the geology, natural history and Miwok culture of Point Reyes.

Earthquake Trail – 0.6 miles and 100' Change

0.0 This trailhead is located east of the Visitor Center next to the picnic area. The trail is paved the entire way and wheelchair accessible. The trail has signs and exhibits explaining the great earthquake of 1906.

0.3 Earthquake motion. The Pacific plate jumped 16 feet northward relative to the North American plate as shown by the fence display.

0.6 Back at the trailhead next to the restroom.

Acorn Woodpecker Found on all three hikes.

Kule Loklo Trail – 0.7 miles and 50' Change

0.0 This trail starts about 100 yds. north of the Visitor Center and climbs slightly to a grove of eucalyptus. Notice the woodpecker holes drilled in dead snags for storing acorns.

0.3 Kule Loklo village. This reconstruction of a Coast Miwok village was started in 1976 and continues today. Cultural demonstrations, work parties and festivals are held here every year. Check with the Visitor Center for a schedule of events.

0.4 Restroom and junction. For a longer way back, you can bear right to pick up the Horse trail as it circles the pasture adding 0.5 miles to the hike. Otherwise, head left and retrace your steps.

0.7 Back at the trailhead north of the Visitor Center.

Morgan - Woodpecker Trails – 0.8 miles and 150' Change

0.0 Start at the main Bear Valley trailhead located at the south end of the parking lot. Take the Morgan trail east as it parallels the road up to the red buildings of the Morgan horse ranch.

0.1 Junction and museum. For an interesting side trip, you can tour the museum that explains the history and workings of the Morgan horse ranch. After that, head left and follow the Woodpecker trail as it skirts the meadow under a canopy of oaks and bays.

0.8 Bear Valley trailhead and Visitor Center.

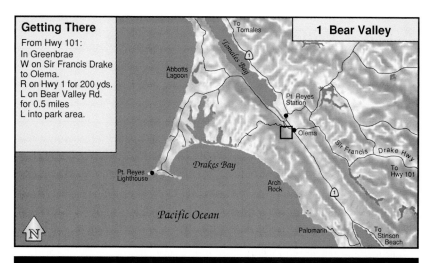

Getting There

From Hwy 101:
In Greenbrae
W on Sir Francis Drake
to Olema.
R on Hwy 1 for 200 yds.
L on Bear Valley Rd.
for 0.5 miles
L into park area.

1 Bear Valley

To
Tomales

Tomales Bay

Abbotts
Lagoon

Pt. Reyes
Station

Olema

Sir Francis   Drake Hwy

To
Hwy 101

Pt. Reyes
Lighthouse

Drakes Bay

Arch
Rock

To
Stinson
Beach

Palomarin

Pacific Ocean

N

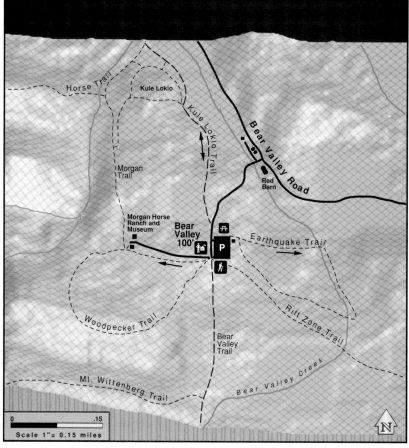

Horse Trail

Kule Loklo

Kule Loklo Trail

Bear Valley Road

Morgan
Trail

Red
Barn

Morgan Horse
Ranch and
Museum

**Bear
Valley
100'**

P

Earthquake Trail

Woodpecker Trail

Rift Zone Trail

Bear
Valley
Trail

Mt. Wittenberg Trail

Bear Valley Creek

0   .15

Scale 1" = 0.15 miles

N

2 Bear Valley - Meadow - Horse Trails

Distance: 6.1 miles   Shaded: 70%
Elevation Change: 1300'   Steep in parts.
Rating: Hiking - 9   Can be dusty in fall.
When to Go: Good anytime, best on clear days in spring.
This hike makes a round trip to the top of Mt. Wittenberg and back.
Great views when clear and good wildflowers in May and June.

0.0 Start at the Bear Valley trailhead south of the parking area.

0.8 Junction #1 with the Meadow trail. Cross the bridge to the right and notice the fallen bay tree straddling the creek. The bay, or California laurel, is very adaptable. It can grow in sun or shade and, when downed, often starts new shoots. Although there are occasional bay trees here, this is primarily a Douglas fir forest.

1.5 The meadow of the Meadow trail. On the right, you can see the deer-graze line about three feet up on the fir trees. At the north end of the meadow, a fir tree, loaded with cones, provides food for squirrels and seeds for new trees. Douglas fir seeds germinate and survive only when they root in mineral soil and receive direct sunlight. These conditions often occur following a fire. Deer, which are common here, munch new seedlings and help maintain the meadow.

Mule Deer

The trail reenters the forest and circles a huge bowl-shaped canyon on the left. The understory is lush with huckleberry, sword fern, tanoak and elderberry.

2.3 Two junctions #2. Head right on the Mt. Wittenberg trail. At this point, the trail leaves the forest and enters an open hillside. Up ahead, the trail provides great views of Drakes Bay and the Point Reyes headlands. You can also see evidence of the 1995 fire.

2.7 Junction #3. Take the trail uphill to the top of Mt. Wittenberg for views of Olema Valley. After exploring the hilltop, return here.

3.1 Junction #3. Take the Z Ranch trail right.

3.8 Junction. Take the Horse trail right downhill.

5.6 Bridge and junction #4. Go left 100 yds., then right into Kule Loklo. Head for the large mound and the road through the eucalyptus.

6.1 Bear Valley trailhead. Water and restrooms.

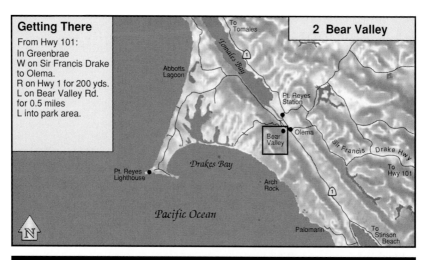

Getting There

From Hwy 101:
In Greenbrae
W on Sir Francis Drake
to Olema.
R on Hwy 1 for 200 yds.
L on Bear Valley Rd.
for 0.5 miles
L into park area.

To
Tomales

Tomales Bay

Abbotts
Lagoon

Pt. Reyes
Station

Bear
Valley

Olema

Sir Francis Drake Hwy

To
Hwy 101

Drakes Bay

Pt. Reyes
Lighthouse

Arch
Rock

Pacific Ocean

Palomarin

To
Stinson
Beach

N

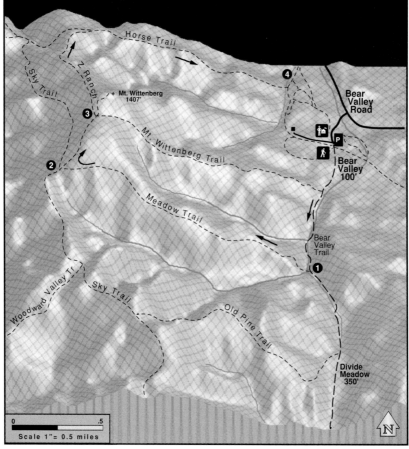

Horse Trail

Sky Trail

Z Ranch

Mt. Wittenberg
1407'

3

Mt. Wittenberg Trail

2

Meadow Trail

Woodwad Valley Tr

Sky Trail

Old Pine Trail

4

Bear
Valley
Road

P

Bear
Valley
100'

Bear
Valley
Trail

1

Divide
Meadow
350'

0   .5

Scale 1"= 0.5 miles

N

3 Bear Valley - Old Pine - Mt. Wittenberg

Distance: 7.3 miles   Shaded: 80%
Elevation Change: 1300'   Steep downhill.
Rating: Hiking - 10
When to Go: Excellent anytime, best from March to June.
This is the best and easiest hike to Inverness Ridge. It provides great views, forest vegetation, good berries and spring wildflowers.

0.0 Start at the Bear Valley trailhead at the south end of the parking area and head into the meadow. Most of the grasses are non-native, imported from Mediterranean countries to feed livestock.

1.0 About 300 yds. past the junction to the Meadow trail, just before starting uphill, there are two interesting plants growing along the left bank, trillium and wild ginger. Trillium has three symmetrical leaves and in late February and March, produces a beautiful flower with three white petals. Ginger has a dark-green, heart-shaped leaf, and from March to June produces deep-purple flowers that are hidden beneath the leaves.

Wild Ginger

1.6 Divide Meadow and junction #1. Take the Old Pine trail right, which provides the easiest climb to the crest of Inverness Ridge. Although called "Old Pine Trail", the trail passes through a magnificent Douglas fir forest.

2.5 Huckleberry lane. Winter rains and summer fog create a luxurious understory, dominated by tall huckleberry shrubs. The small black, edible berries are ripe for picking in August and September.

3.5 Junction #2 with the Sky trail. Head right, to the north.

3.8 Junction with the Woodward Valley trail. In spring, this verdant meadow, edged with firs offers a peaceful rest stop and picnic area.

4.5 Two junctions #3. The trail leaves the forest here; continue straight on the Mt. Wittenberg trail.

4.9 Junction #4 with the Z Ranch trail. If the weather is clear, head uphill to Mt. Wittenberg for dramatic views. Good wildflowers in May.

5.1 Mt. Wittenberg, at 1407'. Often, you will see deer grazing the hillside to the south. Fifty years ago, the entire hilltop was grass. Now, Douglas fir trees are moving in.

5.3 Junction #4. Take the Mt. Wittenberg trail left downhill.

7.3 Back at the Bear Valley trailhead. Water and restrooms.

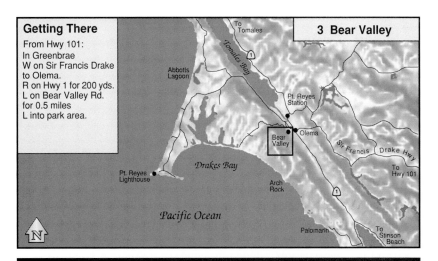

Getting There

From Hwy 101:
In Greenbrae
W on Sir Francis Drake
to Olema.
R on Hwy 1 for 200 yds.
L on Bear Valley Rd.
for 0.5 miles
L into park area.

To Tomales

Tomales Bay

Abbotts Lagoon

Pt. Reyes Station

Bear Valley

Olema

Sir Francis Drake Hwy

To Hwy 101

Pt. Reyes Lighthouse

Drakes Bay

Arch Rock

Pacific Ocean

Palomarin

To Stinson Beach

N

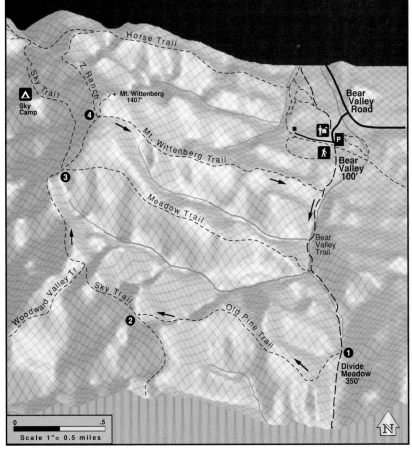

Horse Trail

Sky Trail

Z Ranch

Sky Camp

+ Mt. Wittenberg 1407'

❹

Mt. Wittenberg Trail

❸

Meadow Trail

Bear Valley Road

Bear Valley 100'

P

Bear Valley Trail

Woodward Valley Tr.

Sky Trail

❷

Old Pine Trail

❶

Divide Meadow 350'

0   .5
Scale 1"= 0.5 miles

N

4 Bear Valley Trail to Arch Rock

Distance: 8.2 miles   Shaded: 70%
Elevation Change: 400'
Rating: Hiking - 10   Bicycles allowed part way.
When to Go: Excellent anytime. Best when the coast is clear.
This is the most popular hike on Point Reyes. It is an out and back
hike so you can turn around anytime. Great views at Arch Rock.

0.0 Start at the main trailhead south of the parking area.

1.6 Junction #1 at Divide Meadow. In the early 1890s, the Pacific
Union Club of San Francisco built a sportsman's lodge here with 35
rooms, stables and kennels. The original plans included a golf course,
tennis courts and swimming pool.
Fortunately, the entire resort was
never built. The lodge building
deteriorated and was removed in
1950. You might be able to discover
its location on the east side of the
meadow hilltop. Look for amaryllis
and other plantings nearby.

3.1 Junction #2 with the Glen and
Baldy trails. Bicycles stop here.
Continue towards the ocean.

Bear Valley Country Club ca. 1895

4.0 Junction with the Coast trail. Head north along the Coast trail for
100 yds. and then take the trail to Arch Rock.

4.1 Arch Rock overlook with great views of the coast. To the south,
you can see along Wildcat Beach to Double Point. To the north, you
can see Drakes Bay and the Point Reyes headlands.

4.1 Side trip down near the beach. About 50' from the overlook, a
short, well-used trail drops steeply down to Coast Creek and out to
the beach and ocean. It is worth the trip down to glimpse the sea
tunnel (the "arch" of Arch Rock) where the creek meets the ocean.

If conditions are right - low tide, calm ocean and low creek flow - the
adventurous hiker can cross the creek and explore the small beach
below Arch Rock. **Note:** Proceed with caution and at your own risk!
This is not a park trail. The crossing can be slippery and dangerous.
Also be aware of the tide. Do not get yourself trapped on the beach.
When you are ready to return, retrace your steps.

8.2 Bear Valley trailhead and Visitor Center.

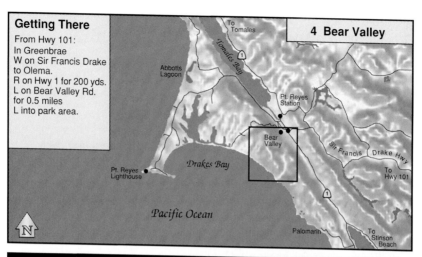

Getting There

From Hwy 101:
In Greenbrae
W on Sir Francis Drake
to Olema.
R on Hwy 1 for 200 yds.
L on Bear Valley Rd.
for 0.5 miles
L into park area.

To Tomales

Tomales Bay

Abbotts
Lagoon

Pt. Reyes
Station

Bear
Valley

Sir Francis   Drake   Hwy

To
Hwy 101

Pt. Reyes
Lighthouse

Drakes Bay

Pacific Ocean

Palomarin

To
Stinson
Beach

N

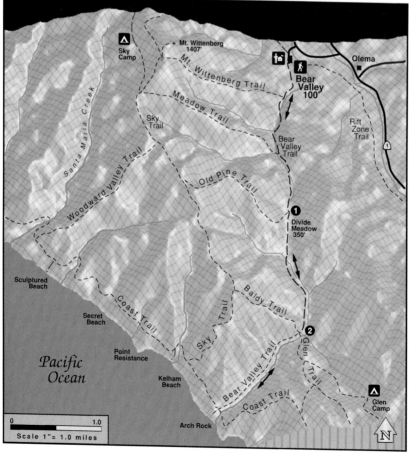

Sky
Camp

+ Mt. Wittenberg
1407'

Mt. Wittenberg Trail

Meadow Trail

Sky
Trail

Bear
Valley
100'

Olema

Rift
Zone
Trail

Bear
Valley
Trail

Santa Maria Creek

Woodward Valley Trail

Old Pine Trail

1

Divide
Meadow
350'

Sculptured
Beach

Coast Trail

Sky Trail

Baldy Trail

Secret
Beach

Point
Resistance

*Pacific
Ocean*

Kelham
Beach

Bear Valley Trail

Coast Trail

Glen Trail

2

Glen
Camp

Arch Rock

0   1.0

Scale 1" = 1.0 miles

N

15

5 Bear Valley - Mt. Wittenberg - Sky

Distance: 10.9 miles   Shaded: 60%
Elevation Change: 1500'   Steep in places.
Rating: Hiking - 9   Some mud possible on the ridge.
When to Go: Excellent anytime, best in May.
This hike takes the steepest route to the Inverness Ridge and then follows the ridge to the coast. Great views and magnificent forests.

0.0 Start at the Bear Valley trailhead, south of the parking area.

0.2 Junction #1 with the Mt. Wittenberg trail, which is guarded by a large bay tree. Turn right and set a slow steady pace to climb the moderately steep trail to the ridge. Occasionally, in the open areas, stop and enjoy the views back east across Olema Valley.

2.0 Junction #2. The trail crests Inverness Ridge at 1250' offering spectacular views of Drakes Bay and the headlands with Sky Camp below in the foreground. For a side trip, you can climb to the top of Mt. Wittenberg. Otherwise, head left on the Mt. Wittenberg trail.

2.4 Two junctions. Head south on the Sky trail as it enters a dramatic Douglas fir forest kept refreshingly moist by winter rains and summer fog. The luxuriant understory is filled with ferns, elderberry, hedge nettle and huckleberry.

3.2 Junction #3 with the Woodward Valley trail. Continue south past this picturesque meadow edged with Douglas fir. Over the next half-mile, look for gooseberry, elderberry, huckleberry and thimbleberry.

Coyote Bush

4.9 Junction #4 with the Baldy trail. Continue straight. Before the Mt. Vision fire, this area produced dense stands of coyote bush. Coyote bush, called "fuzzy wuzzy" because of the white fluff produced on the seeds of the female plant in early summer, dominates the coastal scrub community. Other plants in this "soft chaparral" community include coffeeberry, blackberry, poison oak and sword fern. This is a good place to find brush rabbits, wrentits and the white-crowned sparrow. Up ahead, the trail descends towards the ocean with good views of Pt. Resistance.

6.2 Junction #5. Take the Coast trail left.

6.9 Junction #6. Head right to explore Arch Rock. (See Hike 4 for details.) The hike continues left on the Bear Valley trail.

10.9 Bear Valley trailhead with full facilities.

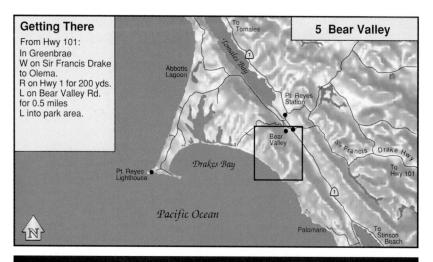

Getting There

From Hwy 101:
In Greenbrae
W on Sir Francis Drake
to Olema.
R on Hwy 1 for 200 yds.
L on Bear Valley Rd.
for 0.5 miles
L into park area.

To
Tomales

Tomales Bay

Abbotts
Lagoon

Pt. Reyes
Station

Bear
Valley

Sir Francis   Drake Hwy

To
Hwy 101

Pt. Reyes
Lighthouse

Drakes Bay

Palomarin

To
Stinson
Beach

Pacific Ocean

N

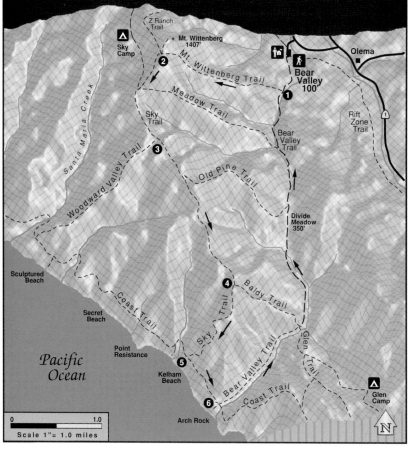

Z Ranch
Trail

Mt. Wittenberg
1407'

Sky
Camp

Mt. Wittenberg Trail

Meadow Trail

Olema

Bear
Valley
100'

❶

Sky
Trail

Santa Maria Creek

Bear
Valley
Trail

Rift
Zone
Trail

Woodward Valley Trail

❸

Old Pine Trail

Divide
Meadow
350'

Sculptured
Beach

Coast Trail

❹

Baldy Trail

Secret
Beach

Sky Trail

Glen Trail

Point
Resistance

Pacific
Ocean

❺

Kelham Beach

Bear Valley Trail

❻

Coast Trail

Arch Rock

Glen
Camp

❷

0   1.0

Scale 1"= 1.0 miles

N

6 Bear Valley - Glen Camp - Coast Trails

Distance: 11.6 miles   Shaded: 70%
Elevation Change: 950'   Steep downhill.
Rating: Hiking - 10   Can be standing water when wet.
When to Go: Excellent anytime, best when calm and clear.

This is one of the premier hikes on Point Reyes that includes a riparian corridor, lush forest, breathtaking views and spring flowers.

0.0 Start at the Bear Valley trailhead, south of the parking area.

0.5 Floods and alders. People still talk about the storm of 1982. Bear Valley was completely blocked by flood debris and over one-half of the trail was destroyed. One of the few remaining signs of the flood are groves of young red alders that seeded the following spring. In time, these alders will get much larger, once again shading the trail.

3.1 Junction #1 with Glen trail. Take the Glen trail across the creek and head uphill out of the lush riparian corridor of alder, elderberry, ferns and mosses and into firs, bays, hazelnut, and forget-me-nots.

3.7 Junction #2. Take the Glen Camp Loop trail left. **Option:** You can short-cut the hike by 0.7 miles by staying on the Glen trail.

4.6 Glen Camp with tables and water. This is the prettiest of the backpacking camps, nestled in a small meadow surrounded by oaks and firs. Look for iris under the oaks in spring. Campers will find lots of wildlife, especially at dusk. The trail continues from the west side of the meadow where it begins a moderately steep climb to the ridge.

5.3 Two junctions. Take the second right, the signed Coast/Glen spur trail west towards the ocean.

5.5 Junction #3 with Coast trail. Bear right. You may have to wade through one to two inches of water in winter time. The trail heads north across open coastal grasslands. Watch for deer.

6.0 Junction and seasonal pond. Continue left on the Coast trail.

6.3 Outcropping, wildflowers, picnic spot and viewpoint. As you look north along Drakes Bay, the largest prominence is Pt. Resistance. The trail begins a moderate descent. Down below and further west, look for a breathtaking view south towards Double Point.

7.4 Junction #4 with Arch Rock trail. Head left to explore Arch Rock.

7.5 Arch Rock. (See Hike 4 for details on getting to the beach.) To return, follow the signs back along the Bear Valley trail.

11.6 Bear Valley trailhead and Visitor Center.

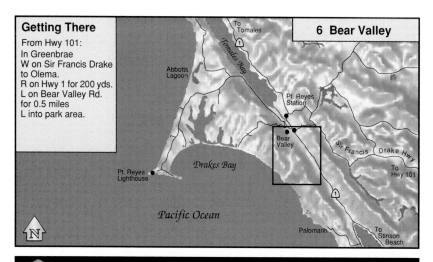

Getting There

From Hwy 101:
In Greenbrae
W on Sir Francis Drake
to Olema.
R on Hwy 1 for 200 yds.
L on Bear Valley Rd.
for 0.5 miles
L into park area.

To Tomales

Tomales Bay

Abbotts Lagoon

Pt. Reyes Station

Bear Valley

Sir Francis Drake Hwy

To Hwy 101

Pt. Reyes Lighthouse

Drakes Bay

Palomarin

To Stinson Beach

Pacific Ocean

N

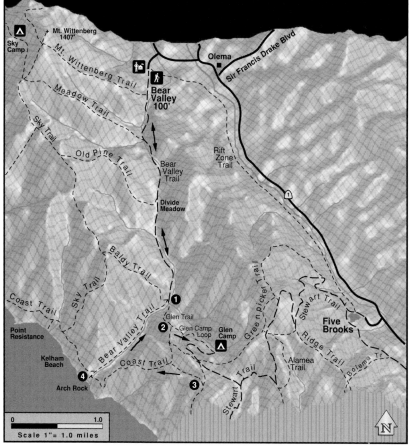

Sky Camp

Mt. Wittenberg 1407'

Mt. Wittenberg Trail

Meadow Trail

Sky Trail

Old Pine Trail

Olema

Sir Francis Drake Blvd

Bear Valley 100'

Bear Valley Trail

Rift Zone Trail

1

Divide Meadow

Baldy Trail

Sky Trail

Bear Valley Trail

Coast Trail

Greenpicker Trail

Stewart Trail

Five Brooks

Point Resistance

❶

Glen Trail

❷ Glen Camp Loop

Glen Camp

Stewart Trail

Ridge Trail

Bolema Trl

Kelham Beach

Coast Trail

Alamea Trail

❹

Arch Rock

❸

0   1.0

Scale 1"= 1.0 miles

N

19

7 Bear Valley - Sky - Woodward Valley

Distance: 12.8 miles   Shaded: 60%
Elevation Change: 1700'   Steep in places.
Rating: Hiking - 10   Can be overgrown. Can be windy.
When to Go: Excellent anytime, best when clear and calm.
This hike has it all! Meadows, forests, creeks, beaches, rolling hills, wildflowers and panoramic views all await the vigorous hiker.

0.0 Start at the Bear Valley trailhead at the south end of the parking area. Look for deer in the meadow, especially in the early morning.

0.2 Junction #1 with the Mt. Wittenberg trail. Head right and start a moderately steep climb under tanoak and Douglas fir.

2.0 Junction #2. The trail crests Inverness Ridge offering dramatic views over Sky Camp to Drakes Bay and the headlands. If the weather is clear, you can take a short side trip and climb 300' to the top of Mt. Wittenberg. Otherwise, head left on the Mt. Wittenberg trail.

2.4 Two junctions. Head south on the Sky trail as it enters a dense Douglas fir forest. In the understory, lush, light-green elderberry presents a striking contrast to the tall, dark fir canopy.

3.2 Junction #3 with Woodward Valley trail. Turn right and head west to follow the trail as it rolls downhill through meadow, forest and open coastal ridges. Tall grass crowds the trail in summer.

4.1 Ocean views. The trail levels off along a rocky outcrop above the ocean. This scenic viewpoint offers a panoramic sweep from the Point Reyes headlands to Double Point.

5.2 Junction #4 with Coast trail. Bear left and head south.

7.7 Kelham Beach access trail. Continue south on the Coast trail. **Option:** In the summer and fall, at tides below plus one foot, the adventurous hiker can walk along Kelham Beach and take the sea tunnel up to Arch Rock. (See Hike 4 for more details).

8.7 Junction #5 with Arch Rock trail. Head right.

8.8 Arch Rock. (See Hike 4 for exploring Arch Rock.) To complete the hike, follow the Bear Valley trail inland as it parallels the creek.

9.0 Buckeye trees. Two large, gnarled buckeyes with twisted trunks stand guard along the right of the trail. Buckeyes produce fragrant flowers in late spring, then soon after, in early summer, begin losing their leaves. The seed is large, brown and shiny like a buck's eye.

12.8 Bear Valley trailhead. Visitor Center, water and restrooms.

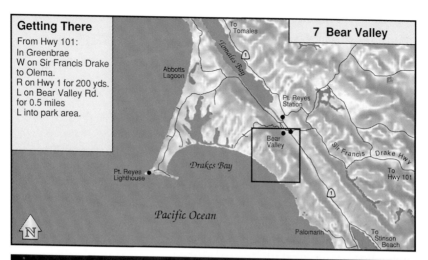

Getting There

From Hwy 101:
In Greenbrae
W on Sir Francis Drake
to Olema.
R on Hwy 1 for 200 yds.
L on Bear Valley Rd.
for 0.5 miles
L into park area.

To Tomales

Tomales Bay

Abbotts Lagoon

Pt. Reyes Station

Bear Valley

Sir Francis Drake Hwy

To Hwy 101

Pt. Reyes Lighthouse

Drakes Bay

Pacific Ocean

Palomarin

To Stinson Beach

N

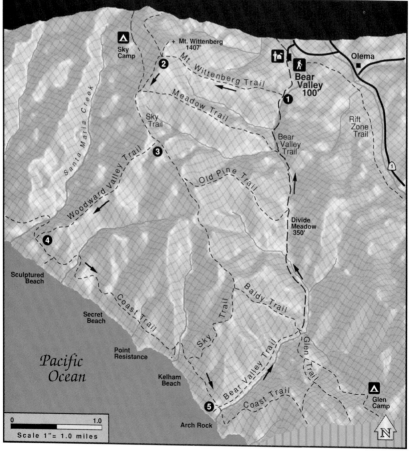

Sky Camp

+ Mt. Wittenberg 1407'

Mt. Wittenberg Trail

Olema

Bear Valley 100'

1

Meadow Trail

Sky Trail

Santa Maria Creek

Bear Valley Trail

Rift Zone Trail

2

3

Woodward Valley Trail

Old Pine Trail

Divide Meadow 350'

4

Sculptured Beach

Secret Beach

Coast Trail

Sky Trail

Baldy Trail

Point Resistance

Pacific Ocean

Kelham Beach

Bear Valley Trail

Glen Trail

Glen Camp

5

Coast Trail

Arch Rock

0   1.0

Scale 1"= 1.0 miles

N

21

8 Olema Valley - Bolema - Stewart

Distance: 6.2 miles   Shaded: 90%
Elevation Change: 1100'   Horses likely.
Rating: Hiking - 9   Can be dusty or muddy.
When to Go: Best in spring, good anytime.

This hike makes a loop around the eastern side of Inverness Ridge through a dense Douglas fir forest.

0.0 Start at the Five Brooks trailhead and take the main trail northwest past the old logging pond towards Inverness Ridge.

0.2 Junction #1. Take the Olema Valley trail left around the pond 100 yds., then bear right at the second junction. The trail heads south through an enchanting forest of Douglas fir, bay and alder with a dense understory of ferns, hazelnut, ginger, nettles and blackberry.

Up ahead, the trail crosses a bridge, then starts a moderately steep climb in more open forest.

1.4 Junction #2. Head right on the Bolema trail and continue to climb. Farther up the trail, you'll see the first stand of Monterey pines that were seeded after logging operations in the late 1950s.

2.5 Junction #3, and the highest point of the hike at 1180'. Head right on the Ridge trail. Occasionally, you get glimpses west to the ocean.

3.1 Forest and berries. The trail enters a dark Douglas fir forest with lots of huckleberries that ripen from July through September. The forest is often damp in the summertime due to heavy fog drip.

3.2 Junction #4. The Ridge trail goes left. Continue straight here and right at the next junction 100 yds. ahead.

3.3 Junction. Take the Stewart trail downhill to the right. The old roadbed was once paved and wide enough for two lanes of traffic. Watch for an occasional large, old-growth Douglas fir on the edge of the roadbed. These trees were left by loggers to support the road and to provide seeds for future trees.

5.2 Junction #5 with the Greenpicker trail. Continue downhill. Up ahead, the trail makes a large hairpin turn in a steep canyon and creek. Look for five-finger ferns along the bank. In June, an aralia with large 12" leaves, and even larger flower stalks, blooms along the moist banks.

6.0 Junction #1 and mill pond. Head left.

6.2 Trailhead with picnic tables, water and restrooms.

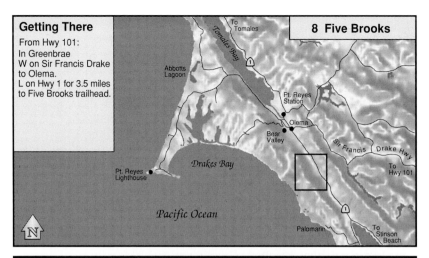

Getting There

From Hwy 101:
In Greenbrae
W on Sir Francis Drake
to Olema.
L on Hwy 1 for 3.5 miles
to Five Brooks trailhead.

8 Five Brooks

To Tomales
Tomales Bay
1
Abbotts Lagoon
Pt. Reyes Station
Olema
Bear Valley
Sir Francis Drake Hwy
To Hwy 101
Drakes Bay
Pt. Reyes Lighthouse
Pacific Ocean
1
Palomarin
To Stinson Beach
N

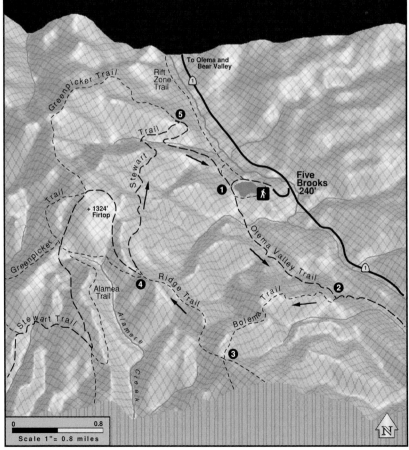

To Olema and Bear Valley
1
Rift Zone Trail
Greenpicker Trail
Trail
Stewart
Trail
Greenpicker
+ 1324' Firtop
Trail
Greenpicker
Alamea Trail
Stewart Trail
Alamere Creek
Ridge Trail
Five Brooks 240'
Olema Valley Trail
1
Bolema Trail

0   0.8
Scale 1"= 0.8 miles
N

9 Stewart - Greenpicker Trails

Distance: 7.5 miles   Shaded: 90%
Elevation Change: 1300'   Moderately steep in places.
Rating: Hiking - 7   Dusty when dry. Bicycles possible.
When to Go: Good anytime, best in February and March.

This hike stays entirely in a scenic Douglas fir forest as it climbs the eastern slopes of Inverness Ridge.

0.0 Start at the Five Brooks parking area and head northwest through the gate. Circle the pond bordered by willows and alders.

0.2 Junction #1 with the Olema Valley and Stewart trails. Head right and follow the signs to Firtop. The Stewart trail is really a wide road that makes a moderate climb through a Douglas fir forest with occasional bay, alder and tanoak. Ferns and elderberry dominate the understory.

Five-finger Fern

0.7 Hairpin turn. Just past the turn, look for four different ferns on the steep bank - lady fern, sword fern, five-finger fern and chain fern.

1.0 Junction with the Greenpicker trail. Continue left towards Firtop. Up ahead, you'll find stumps of Douglas fir, remnants of the logging operations that ended in the late 1950s.

2.9 Junction #2 with the Ridge trail. Continue on the Stewart trail.

3.7 Junction and Firtop at 1324'. The small meadow at Firtop is surrounded by firs, blocking what were once magnificent views. You can cut the hike short by returning on the Greenpicker trail. Otherwise, continue across the meadow and head downhill.

4.0 Two junctions #3. Go right about 100' on the Ridge trail and pick up the Greenpicker trail to head back towards Five Brooks. The trail first makes a moderate descent for 0.2 miles, then climbs steeply through a very dense forest back up to Firtop.

4.7 Junction #4 with the spur trail to Stewart trail. Continue left on the Greenpicker trail. This part of the hike borders the private property of the Vedanta Society. Up ahead, the terrain becomes more difficult and leaves the road to enter an old growth forest with lots of huckleberries and sword ferns.

6.5 Junction. Head left, downhill on the Stewart trail.

7.5 Five Brooks trailhead with water and restrooms.

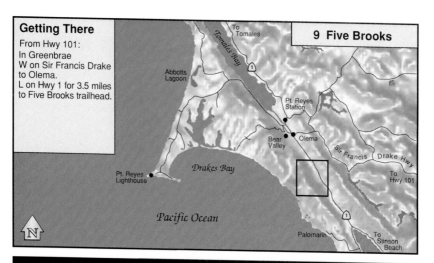

Getting There

From Hwy 101:
In Greenbrae
W on Sir Francis Drake
to Olema.
L on Hwy 1 for 3.5 miles
to Five Brooks trailhead.

To Tomales

Tomales Bay

Abbotts
Lagoon

Pt. Reyes
Station

Bear
Valley

Olema

Sir Francis Drake Hwy

To
Hwy 101

Pt. Reyes
Lighthouse

Drakes Bay

Pacific Ocean

Palomarin

To
Stinson
Beach

N

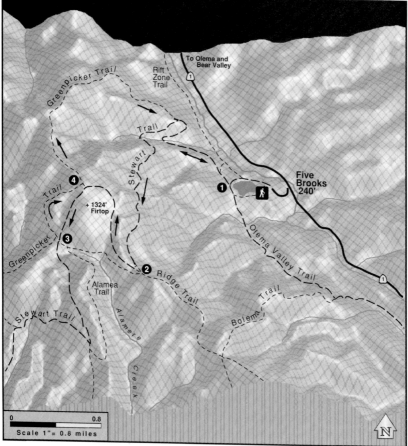

Greenpicker Trail

To Olema and
Bear Valley

Rift
Zone
Trail

Stewart Trail

Trail

4

Trail

+ 1324'
Firtop

1

Five
Brooks
240'

3

Greenpicker

2

Ridge Trail

Olema Valley Trail

Alamea
Trail

Alamere

Bolema Trail

Stewart Trail

Creek

0   0.8

Scale 1"= 0.8 miles

N

25

10 Greenpicker - Coast - Stewart Trails

Distance: 10.8 miles   Shaded: 70%
Elevation Change: 1600'   Bicycles possible on Stewart trail.
Rating: Hiking - 8   Poison oak may crowd Coast trail.
When to Go: Good anytime, best when clear.

This is a rugged hike that makes a moderately steep climb through dense forest, then provides dramatic views along the coast.

0.0 Start at the Five Brooks parking area and circle the pond bordered by willows and alders. Look for ducks and turtles.

0.2 Junction #1. Head right on the Stewart trail.

1.0 Junction #2. Take the Greenpicker trail right as it heads uphill, then skirts the private Vedanta property. The trail climbs through rugged terrain that supports a luxuriant Douglas fir forest. The tall canopy allows light for a dense growth of ferns and huckleberry.

2.8 Junction with the Stewart trail and Firtop at 1324'. A spur trail leads left to the meadow at Firtop. Continue on the Greenpicker trail.

3.5 Junction #3 with Ridge and Stewart trails. Continue on the Greenpicker trail as it goes right downhill.

4.5 Junction #4 with Glen trail. Go left up the road.

4.6 Two junctions. Take the second right, the Coast Spur trail.

4.8 Junction with Coast trail. Head left. Watch out for poison oak.

5.1 Wildcat Camp overlook. Here is one of the premier viewing spots on Point Reyes. The wild-looking, jumbled hills from Wildcat Camp to Bass Lake are mostly the result of massive landslides. See if you can spot evidence of old scarps, large cuts and slides on the western slopes of Inverness Ridge.

5.7 Junction #5 with the Stewart trail. Bear left. **Option**: Head right for 0.7 miles for a side trip to Wildcat Camp and the beach.

6.2 Junction with Glen trail. Stay right on the Stewart trail.

6.5 Two uncommon shrubs. Just 20' past an exposed cliff, look for a white ceanothus, which flowers in May and below it, a silk tassel shrub, with hanging catkins. Both plants are seldom seen on Point Reyes. Continue on the Stewart trail.

7.4 Junction #3. Take the Ridge trail right to circle Firtop.

7.9 Junction #6. Head left 200' to pick up the Stewart trail.

10.8 Five Brooks trailhead with water and restrooms.

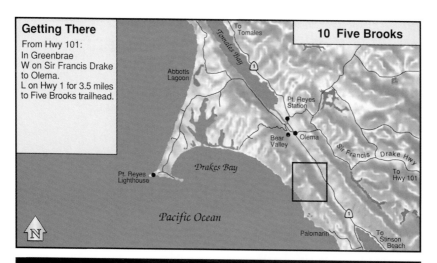

Getting There

From Hwy 101:
In Greenbrae
W on Sir Francis Drake
to Olema.
L on Hwy 1 for 3.5 miles
to Five Brooks trailhead.

10 Five Brooks

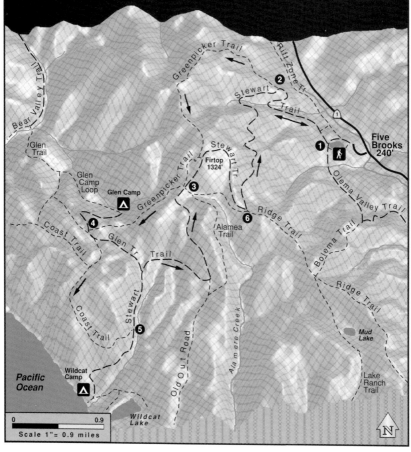

27

11 Randall - Olema Valley - Bolema

Distance: 9.8 miles   Shaded: 70%
Elevation Change: 1200'   Steep and rutted in places.
Rating: Hiking - 7   Trail may be closed. See Note.
When to Go: Best in April and May after the ground dries a bit.
This loop hike follows the earthquake terrain of Olema Valley, then
climbs the heavily forested Inverness Ridge.

Note: The Teixeira trail can be steep with exposed roots and deep
ruts. It has often been closed. Check with the Visitor Center before
going. Also, see the note for Hike 35 about the Olema Valley trail.

0.0 Start at the Randall trailhead located near mile marker 20.53 on
Highway 1. Take the Randall Spur trail west along a bank of willows
heading towards Inverness Ridge. Look for warblers in the willows.

0.4 Junction #1. Head right on the Olema Valley trail and start a
gentle climb through a mixture of open grassland and oak, bay, and fir
trees. The trail can be muddy or dusty depending on the season.

Occasionally, look back to view the jumbled topography of the San
Andreas rift zone. It is estimated that the Inverness Ridge to the west
is moving 1.3" per year relative to the Bolinas Ridge to the east. This
motion adds up to more than 1000' over the last 10,000 years.

1.7 Junction #2 with the Bolema trail. Head left to climb the old ranch
road towards the ridge. This is mostly Douglas fir forest with ferns,
hazelnut, hedge nettle and thimbleberries in the understory.

2.8 Junction #3. Take the Ridge trail left and head south on the ridge.

3.1 Tree stumps and succession. Clearcut logging along the ridge in
the late 1950s opened the way for manzanita to establish itself. Now,
the second generation firs have formed a dense canopy shading out
the manzanita and causing dieback.

5.3 Junction #4. Take the Teixeira trail left. Watch for stinging nettles.

6.0 Junction with the Pablo Point trail. Continue downhill on the
Teixeira trail. Ahead, trail conditions deteriorate as horses and water
have created deep ruts with exposed roots and jagged rocks.

7.1 Junction #5. The trail crosses a bog right before the junction. (A
bypass trail can be taken around the bog 0.1 mile before the junction.)
Head left on the Olema Valley trail through an open meadow.

9.4 Junction. Take the Randall Spur trail east.

9.8 Back at the trailhead. If grass crowded the trail, check for ticks.

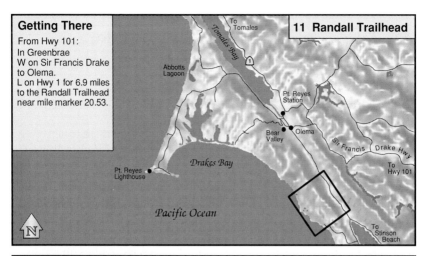

Getting There
From Hwy 101:
In Greenbrae
W on Sir Francis Drake
to Olema.
L on Hwy 1 for 6.9 miles
to the Randall Trailhead
near mile marker 20.53.

To
Tomales

Tomales Bay

Abbotts
Lagoon

Pt. Reyes
Station

Bear
Valley

Olema

Sir Francis Drake Hwy

To
Hwy 101

Drakes Bay

Pt. Reyes
Lighthouse

Pacific Ocean

To
Stinson
Beach

N

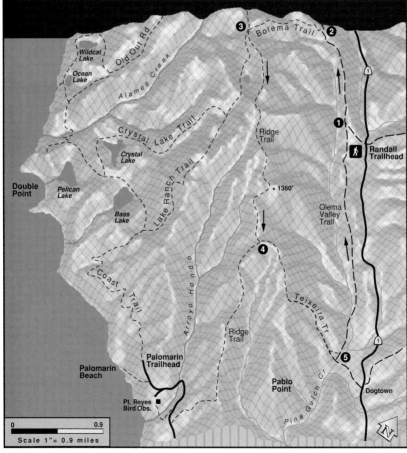

Wildcat
Lake

Old Out Rd

Ocean
Lake

Alamea Creek

Bolema Trail

3

2

1

Crystal Lake Trail

Ridge
Trail

Randall
Trailhead

Crystal
Lake

Double
Point

Pelican
Lake

Lake Ranch Trail

+ 1360'

Olema
Valley
Trail

Bass
Lake

Coast Trail

Arroyo Hondo

4

Teixeira Tr.

Ridge
Trail

5

Palomarin
Trailhead

Palomarin
Beach

Pablo
Point

Dogtown

Pt. Reyes
Bird Obs.

Pine Gulch Cr.

N

0   0.9

Scale 1"= 0.9 miles

29

12 PRBO and Palomarin Beach Trails

Distance: 0.5 and 0.8 miles   Shaded: 60% and 10%
Elevation Change: 250' for the Palomarin Beach trail.
Rating: Hiking - 10   Both trails moderately steep.
When to Go: Excellent anytime, beach trail best at low tide.

The Point Reyes Bird Observatory Nature trail explores a magnificent small canyon with dense growth. The beach trail leads to tidepools.

Point Reyes Bird Observatory Nature Trail – 0.5 miles and 50'

Note: A trail pamphlet is available at the PRBO Visitor Center.

0.0 Start at the PRBO parking lot and take the nature trail south past coyote bush and wind-pruned fir trees. At 100 yds., notice the tough, scrub oak trees growing close to the ground.

Up ahead, the trail heads steeply down into Fern Canyon guarded by twisted buckeye trees covered with old man's beard, a grey-green lichen hanging in the branches. This little canyon provides a rain forest habitat of robust flora and noisy birds. Look for several kinds of ferns and berries – sword fern, five-finger fern, chain fern, blackberries and thimbleberries – under a canopy of buckeye trees.

0.1 The trail crosses the creek and climbs out the other side. A multi-trunked buckeye stands over patches of Solomon's seal.

Continue across the bluff to a 4-way junction marked by three posts on your left. If the trail is not overgrown with blackberries and thimbleberries, head left through the posts to the road. Otherwise retrace your steps.

0.2 Road. Go left past the exposed shale cliffs.

0.5 Entrance to PRBO.

Palomarin Beach Trail – 0.8 miles and 250' Change

0.0 Start at the trailhead 0.3 miles north of the Point Reyes Bird Observatory. Follow the trail as it heads down past eucalyptus, sage and coastal scrub towards the beach. Look for wildflowers in spring. Up ahead, a sign cautions visitors to watch for slippery rocks and large waves. This spot also offers great views south down the coast and northwest across Drakes Bay to the Point Reyes headlands.

0.3 Hollow. The trail skirts the edge of a wet hollow, then drops down to the beach.

0.4 Beach. You can explore in both directions from here.

0.8 Parking area.

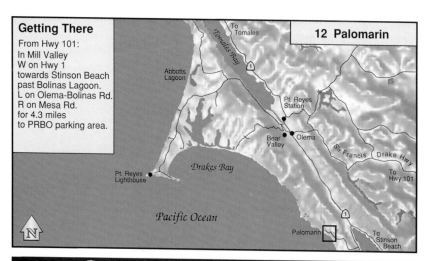

Getting There

From Hwy 101:
In Mill Valley
W on Hwy 1
towards Stinson Beach
past Bolinas Lagoon.
L on Olema-Bolinas Rd.
R on Mesa Rd.
for 4.3 miles
to PRBO parking area.

To
Tomales

Tomales Bay

Abbotts
Lagoon

Pt. Reyes
Station

Bear
Valley

Olema

Sir Francis

Drake Hwy

To
Hwy 101

Drakes Bay

Pt. Reyes
Lighthouse

Pacific Ocean

Palomarin

To
Stinson
Beach

N

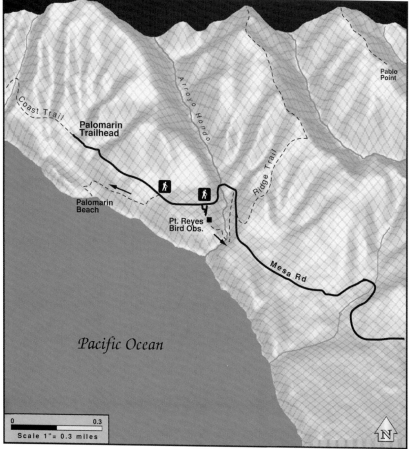

Coast Trail

Arroyo Hondo

Pablo
Point

**Palomarin
Trailhead**

Ridge Trail

**Palomarin
Beach**

Pt. Reyes
Bird Obs.

Mesa Rd

Pacific Ocean

0   0.3
Scale 1"= 0.3 miles

N

13 Coast Trail to Double Point

Distance: 8.0 miles   Shaded: 20%
Elevation Change: 1000'   Steep cliffs at end. Can be windy.
Rating: Hiking - 9   Poison oak may crowd trail in places.
When to Go: Excellent anytime, best from December to July.

Double Point provides one of the best view spots on the west coast. In season, look for whales, seals and wildflowers. Can be windy.

0.0 Start at 260' at the Palomarin parking area. Take the dirt road up towards the eucalyptus grove. In spring, look for lupine, cow parsnip, Indian paintbrush, iris, wild cucumber and poppies.

2.0 Small pass. After heading inland into a large ravine, the trail makes a long climb up through a narrow rocky pass at 580'. These outcroppings of chert, shale and sandstone are marine deposits, part of a sedimentary layer that covers most of the southern seashore.

2.2 Junction #1 with the Lake Ranch Trail. Continue left.

2.7 Bass Lake. The first glimpse through the willows and coyote bush provides an enticing view of this lovely lake.

2.8 Unmarked junction. A spur trail left explores the lake shoreline. On warm days, you'll often find picnickers and swimmers here. The hike continues uphill into a small fir forest where ferns, ceanothus and coffeeberry offer a nice change of pace from the open hillsides.

3.3 Pelican Lake. Across the lake, a small notch between Double Point allows overflow in wet years. Pelican Lake and the lakes in this area were formed by landslides that blocked normal drainage.

3.6 Two junctions #2 (see map – inset). At the first junction at the north end of the lake, take the spur trail left. **Note**: At the second junction 150' beyond, another spur trail goes left 0.5 miles to the top of Alamere Falls. This trail is unmaintained and may be overgrown with poison oak.

4.0 Double Point at 490'. This spot provides commanding views of the coastline and hills inland. (Stay well back from the cliffs edge!) In winter and spring, look for whales in the ocean. Also check the beaches below for harbor seals that breed here from May to July. When done, retrace your steps.

8.0 Palomarin trailhead. Restrooms, but no water.

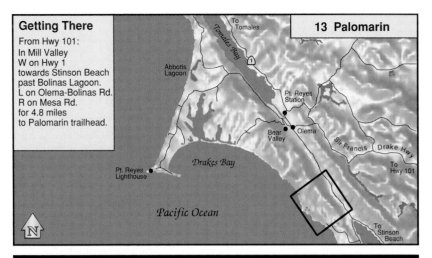

Getting There

From Hwy 101:
In Mill Valley
W on Hwy 1
towards Stinson Beach
past Bolinas Lagoon.
L on Olema-Bolinas Rd.
R on Mesa Rd.
for 4.8 miles
to Palomarin trailhead.

To Tomales

Tomales Bay

Abbotts Lagoon

Pt. Reyes Station

Bear Valley

Olema

Sir Francis Drake Hwy

To Hwy 101

Drakes Bay

Pt. Reyes Lighthouse

Pacific Ocean

To Stinson Beach

N

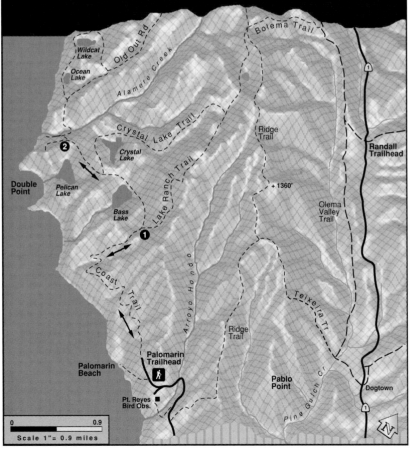

Old Out Rd.

Bolema Trail

Wildcat Lake

Ocean Lake

Alamere Creek

Crystal Lake Trail

Ridge Trail

Randall Trailhead

Crystal Lake

Double Point

Pelican Lake

Lake Ranch Trail

Bass Lake

+ 1360'

Olema Valley Trail

Coast Trail

Arroyo Hondo

Teixeira Tr.

Ridge Trail

Palomarin Trailhead

Palomarin Beach

Pablo Point

Pine Gulch Cr.

Pt. Reyes Bird Obs.

Dogtown

0   0.9

Scale 1"= 0.9 miles

N

14 Ridge - Lake Ranch - Coast Trails

Distance: 11.2 miles   Shaded: 70%
Elevation Change: 1300'   Moderately steep downhill.
Rating: Hiking - 9   Can be muddy. Some poison oak.
When to Go: Excellent anytime, best in spring when clear.

This hike climbs the southern end of Inverness Ridge into a magnificent fir forest, then drops through a massive landslide area.

0.0 Park in the Point Reyes Bird Observatory parking lot. Take the signed Nature trail down into a small canyon featuring luxuriant growth and striking buckeye trees. Cross the creek and immediately head up the other side. Follow the trail across the plateau to a four-way junction marked by three short poles on your left. Head left past the poles and through dense blackberry vines towards the road.

0.2 Junction with Mesa Rd. Head right down the dirt road.

0.4 Junction #1 with the Ridge trail. Turn left and start a moderately steep climb through coastal scrub dotted with wind-pruned Douglas fir. The trail may be overgrown in places. Watch out for poison oak.

1.6 Views. Good views east to Pablo Point and beyond to Bolinas Ridge and south to Bolinas Lagoon.

Up ahead, the trail enters a dense conifer forest that covers the Inverness Ridge from here to Point Reyes Hill ten miles north.

2.7 Junction #2 with the Teixeira trail. Continue north on the ridge.

3.6 Mountain top at 1360'. A large moss-covered Douglas fir stands at the highest point on the southern ridge. This area was heavily logged in the late '50s which allowed manzanita to spread. Now the manzanita is dying out under the shade of the second growth of fir.

5.2 Junction #3. Take the Lake Ranch trail to the left. Up ahead, Mud Lake provides a home to red-winged blackbirds.

6.0 Junction with Crystal Lake trail. Continue on the Lake Ranch trail.

7.1 Views and landslides. The trail heads south into open grassland providing great views of the coast below and of the headlands north. On your left, look for evidence of the massive slides that reshaped the landscape and created a series of ponds and lakes below. For the next mile, try to imagine how these slides took place.

8.3 Junction #4. Head left on the Coast trail.

10.5 Palomarin trailhead #5. Continue on the road south.

11.2 PRBO parking area. No facilities.

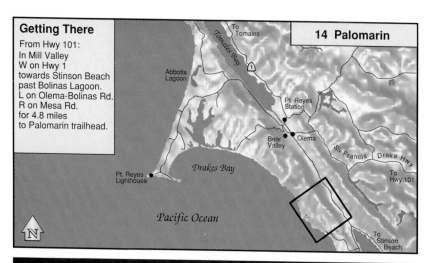

Getting There

From Hwy 101:
In Mill Valley
W on Hwy 1
towards Stinson Beach
past Bolinas Lagoon.
L on Olema-Bolinas Rd.
R on Mesa Rd.
for 4.8 miles
to Palomarin trailhead.

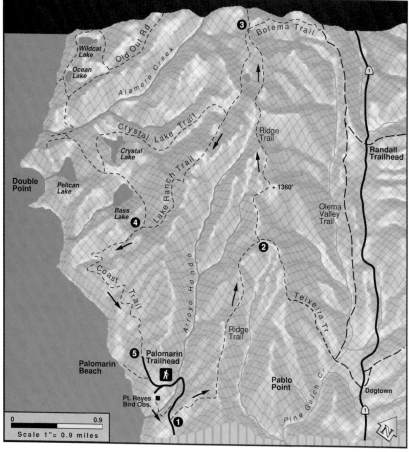

15 Coast Trail to Wildcat Camp

Distance: 11.0 miles   Shaded: 20%
Elevation Change: 1200'
Rating: Hiking - 9   Poison oak along trail in places.
When to Go: Good anytime, best in April and May.

This hike follows the Coast trail past ponds and lakes to Wildcat Camp where you can make a side trip to Alamere Falls. Good views.

0.0 Start at 260' at the Palomarin parking area. Take the dirt road up towards the eucalyptus grove.

0.6 Coastal views. The trail skirts the cliff offering dramatic views both north and south. In spring, the green hills are dotted with blue lupine, white cow parsnip and the red or yellow Indian paintbrush. Other spring wildflowers include iris, wild cucumber and poppy.

2.2 Junction #1 with Lake Ranch trail. Continue left. Up ahead, the trail passes several small ponds formed by slumping soil. All of the ponds and lakes in this area were formed thousands of years ago by massive landslides that blocked normal creek drainage.

2.7 Bass Lake. Coastal scrub edges the southern shore of Point Reyes' most picturesque lake while Douglas fir frames the north side.

2.8 Unmarked junction. A spur trail left explores Bass Lake.

3.3 Pelican Lake. Across the lake, a small notch between Double Point allows an overflow in wet years.

3.6 Three junctions. (See map inset Hike 13.) Continue on Coast trail.

Bass Lake

4.2 Junction #2 with Ocean Lake Loop. Head left. Good views ahead.

5.3 Junction #3 with the Coast trail. Head left.

5.5 Wildcat Camp. Water and restrooms available. Be sure to go down the ravine to the beach for a view south to Alamere Falls.

Option: If the tide is out, walk south along the beach 1.1 miles to the 40' Alamere Falls. Alamere Creek flows all year, but is most spectacular in the spring and after heavy rains.

For the return trip, take the Coast trail south towards Palomarin.

11.0 Palomarin trailhead. Restrooms, but no water.

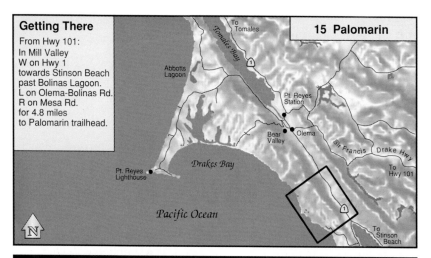

Getting There

From Hwy 101:
In Mill Valley
W on Hwy 1
towards Stinson Beach
past Bolinas Lagoon.
L on Olema-Bolinas Rd.
R on Mesa Rd.
for 4.8 miles
to Palomarin trailhead.

To Tomales
Tomales Bay
Abbotts Lagoon
Pt. Reyes Station
Bear Valley
Olema
Sir Francis Drake Hwy
To Hwy 101
Drakes Bay
Pt. Reyes Lighthouse
Pacific Ocean
To Stinson Beach
N

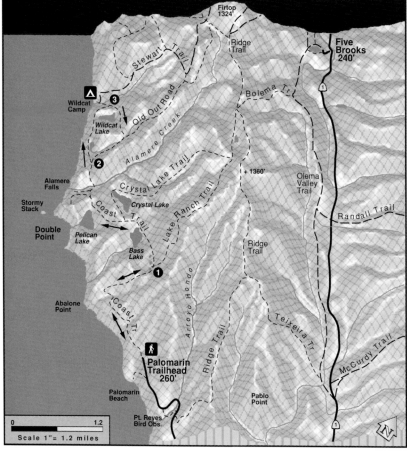

Firtop 1324
Ridge Trail
Five Brooks 240'
Stewart Trail
Bolema Tr.
Wildcat Camp
Wildcat Lake
Old Out Road
Alamere Creek
+ 1360'
Olema Valley Trail
Alamere Falls
Crystal Lake Trail
Lake Ranch Trail
Randall Trail
Stormy Stack
Coast Trail
Crystal Lake
Double Point
Pelican Lake
Ridge Trail
Bass Lake
Arroyo Hondo
Teixeira Tr.
Abalone Point
Coast Tr.
Ridge Trail
Pablo Point
McCurdy Trail
Palomarin Trailhead 260'
Palomarin Beach
Pt. Reyes Bird Obs.

0   1.2
Scale 1"= 1.2 miles

N

16 Sky - Horse - Z Ranch Trails

Distance: 4.6 miles   Shaded: 50%
Elevation Change: 750'
Rating: Hiking - 10   Can be muddy.
When to Go: Excellent anytime, best in late spring.
This is the easiest hike to the top of Mt. Wittenberg. When clear, the hike provides great views in all directions. Good wildflowers in May.

0.0 Start at the Sky trailhead about 3.5 miles out the Limantour Road. The trail is an old ranch road that climbs south through a mostly Douglas fir forest lush with berries, nettles and ferns.

0.8 Junction #1. Take the Horse trail left. At the start of the trail, notice the large patch of salal with bright green, shiny leaves . Up ahead, the trail circles a steep canyon bare of conifers. The canyon's bowl shape suggests that a large slide occurred. In winter, water from a spring seeps out of the hillside, and may cause further soil erosion.

1.2 Junction #2. The vegetation opens up to provide good views north. The large flat mountain due north is Point Reyes Hill at 1336'. Turn right and head uphill on the Z Ranch trail.

1.3 More evidence of slides. The trail doubles back above the large canyon. Here is where the slide must have started. Notice the large firs above the trail. Also, notice there is much less seepage. Up ahead, the view north gets better. You can just get a glimpse of Mt. Saint Helena 40 miles northeast in Sonoma County.

1.9 Junction #3 and more views. Drakes Bay and the Point Reyes headlands provide a nice background to the grassy slopes of Mt. Wittenberg and Sky Camp below. Take the spur trail up to the top of Mt. Wittenberg. Look for tidy tips and lupine in May and June.

2.1 Mt. Wittenberg at 1407'. This is the highest point on Point Reyes. Circle the broad mountain top and enjoy the views before heading back down. Look for deer along the southern hilltops.

2.3 Junction #3. Take the Mt. Wittenberg trail south along the ridge.

2.9 Two junctions #4. Take the Sky trail right towards Sky Camp.

3.3 Sky Camp and spring. To explore the spring take the short spur trail to the left. When done, continue down the road past the restroom.

3.8 Junction #1 and rock exposure. Just before the junction, slabs of sedimentary rock, called Monterey shale, lie exposed along the trail.

4.6 Back at the trailhead. No facilities.

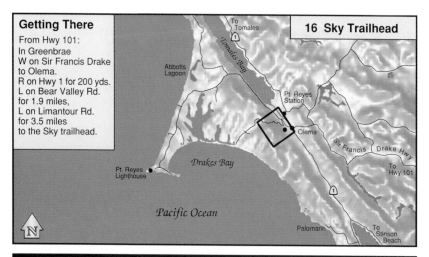

Getting There

From Hwy 101:
In Greenbrae
W on Sir Francis Drake
to Olema.
R on Hwy 1 for 200 yds.
L on Bear Valley Rd.
for 1.9 miles,
L on Limantour Rd.
for 3.5 miles
to the Sky trailhead.

To Tomales

Abbotts Lagoon

Tomales Bay

Pt. Reyes Station

Olema

Sir Francis Drake Hwy

To Hwy 101

Pt. Reyes Lighthouse

Drakes Bay

Pacific Ocean

Palomarin

To Stinson Beach

N

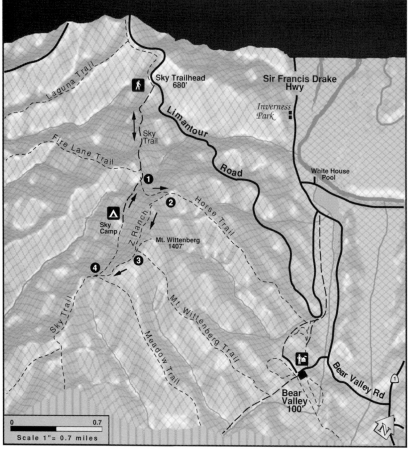

Laguna Trail

Sky Trailhead 680'

Sir Francis Drake Hwy

Inverness Park

Limantour

Sky Trail

Fire Lane Trail

Road

White House Pool

❶

Sky Camp

❷

Z Ranch

Horse Trail

Mt. Wittenberg 1407'

❹

❸

Sky Trail

Mt. Wittenberg Trail

Meadow Trail

Bear Valley Rd

Bear Valley 100'

N

0   0.7
Scale 1" = 0.7 miles

17 Sky - Fire Lane - Laguna Trails

Distance: 6.2 miles   Shaded: 60%
Elevation Change: 1000'   Moderately steep in places.
Rating: Hiking - 9   Can be wet.
When to Go: Good anytime. Try early morning in winter for views.

This trail provides interesting terrain as it rolls down a ridgeline from Mt. Wittenberg. Early morning sunshine makes the headlands glow.

0.0 Start at the Sky trailhead and head uphill on the road. About 200 yds. up the trail, where it breaks into the open, look for Bishop pine to the right of the trail. This is a good hike for comparing Douglas fir and Bishop pine. Douglas fir have small, one-inch needles splayed around a stem. Bishop Pine have two needles per bunch, each three inches long. The cones of the Bishop pine are bigger, harder and heavier. Most of this hike takes place in a transition zone between Douglas fir and Bishop pine communities.

0.8 Junction #1 with Fire Lane trail. Take a right and follow the trail as it skirts the hilltop. The trail climbs slightly to 1090' then starts a moderate descent towards the ocean.

Bishop Pine   *Douglas Fir*

1.0 Great views. The trail descends through a mixture of dead trees, forest and coastal scrub. The dead trees are from the Mt. Vision fire. In open areas, look for great views of the rolling hills, Drakes Bay and the Farallon Islands.

2.0 The trail is deceptive. You expect it to be all downhill, but it climbs several knolls, each one bringing different views.

3.1 Junction #2. Often, you can hear frogs from a marsh 300 yds. to the south. Take the Laguna trail north here. After heavy rains, there may be standing water up ahead. In some places, the trail consists of fine, sandy soil. When the trail is wet, look for animal tracks. **Option:** For a side trip, continue to Coast Camp and the ocean.

3.9 Junction #3 with the road and the ranger residence at 140'. Stay on the Laguna trail as it heads uphill to the right. Notice the large, old buckeye trees with their multiple trunks covered with moss and lichen.

4.2 Junction with the Hidden Valley trail. Continue straight. At the end of the grassy meadow, the trail starts a moderate climb northeast.

5.5 Junction #4 with the Bayview trail. Turn right and head southeast.

6.2 Sky trailhead. No facilities.

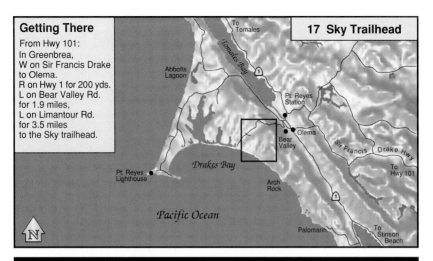

Getting There

From Hwy 101:
In Greenbrea,
W on Sir Francis Drake
to Olema.
R on Hwy 1 for 200 yds.
L on Bear Valley Rd.
for 1.9 miles,
L on Limantour Rd.
for 3.5 miles
to the Sky trailhead.

To Tomales

Tomales Bay

Abbotts Lagoon

1

Pt. Reyes Station

Bear Valley

Olema

Sir Francis Drake Hwy

To Hwy 101

Pt. Reyes Lighthouse

Drakes Bay

Arch Rock

1

Pacific Ocean

Palomarin

To Stinson Beach

N

Bayview Trail

Muddy Hollow Road

Limantour Road

Laguna Trail

④

Sky Trailhead

🚶

Sky Trail

①

Horse Trail

Mt. Wittenberg 1407'

Fire Lane Trail

Muddy Hollow Trailhead

Pt. Reyes Hostel

△ Sky Camp

③

②

Meadow Trail

Santa Maria Creek

Sky Trail

Fire Lane Trail

Woodward Valley Trail

Coast Trail

△ Coast Camp

Drakes Bay

Sculptured Beach

0   .8
Scale 1"= 0.8 miles

N

18 Sky - Woodward Valley - Coast Trails

Distance: 10.7 miles   Shaded: 50%
Elevation Change: 1300'   Steep downhill.
Rating: Hiking - 9   Can be wet in winter, overgrown in summer.
When to Go: Excellent anytime, best when clear and calm.
This hike explores the western slopes of Mt. Wittenberg down to the ocean. It offers a variety of terrain and views, and beach access.

0.0 Start at the Sky trailhead located 3.5 miles out the Limantour Road and take the trail south as it climbs towards Sky Camp.

0.8 Two junctions #1. Continue uphill past both the Fire Lane trail and the Horse trail, which is located 100 yds. farther up the road.

1.2 Sky Camp. Near the restroom, you can climb a small knoll to the right to get good views of Drakes Bay. The trail continues south.

1.8 Two junctions #2. Bear right and head south past the Meadow trail. The Sky trail rolls downhill along the Inverness Ridge and enters a magnificent Douglas fir forest. Huckleberry, elderberry, ferns and nettles make up the lush understory.

2.6 Junction #3 and meadow. Take the Woodward Valley trail as it heads down through the oval-shaped meadow.

4.3 View point. The trail levels off along a rocky outcrop offering commanding views of the coastline. To the south, you can see all the way to Double Point and just below it, Alamere Falls. To the north, you see the sweeping arc of Drakes Bay culminating in the Point Reyes headlands and Chimney Rock.

4.6 Junction. Take the Coast trail north. Up ahead, the trail turns inland to cross Santa Maria Creek, then returns to the coast. Look for a large, granite outcropping high above the trail.

5.3 Coast Camp. Water, restrooms and beach access. **Option:** Take the trail west along the creek to explore the beach.

5.4 Junction #4. Take the Fire Lane trail to the right and start a moderate climb through open grassland. Up ahead, the trail passes a marshy area where you may hear frogs croaking.

6.5 Junction #5. Continue straight on the Laguna trail, which can have standing water in the winter.

8.7 Junction #6. Head right, staying on the Laguna trail.

10.0 Junction. Take the Bayview trail to the right.

10.7 Back at the Sky trailhead. No facilities.

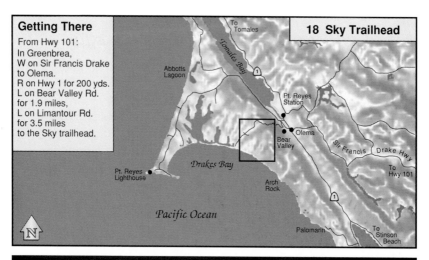

Getting There

From Hwy 101:
In Greenbrea,
W on Sir Francis Drake
to Olema.
R on Hwy 1 for 200 yds.
L on Bear Valley Rd.
for 1.9 miles,
L on Limantour Rd.
for 3.5 miles
to the Sky trailhead.

To Tomales

Tomales Bay

Abbotts Lagoon

Pt. Reyes Station

Olema

Bear Valley

Sir Francis Drake Hwy

To Hwy 101

Pt. Reyes Lighthouse

Drakes Bay

Arch Rock

Palomarin

To Stinson Beach

Pacific Ocean

N

Bayview Trail

Muddy Hollow Road

Limantour Road

Laguna Trail

Fire Lane Trail

Sky Trailhead

Sky Trail

Horse Trail

Muddy Hollow Trailhead

Pt. Reyes Hostel

❶

Sky Camp

Mt. Wittenberg 1407'

❻

❷

Meadow Trail

Santa Maria Creek

❺

❸

Sky Trail

Fire Lane Trail

Woodward Valley Trail

Coast Trail

❹

Coast Camp

Drakes Bay

Sculptured Beach

0   .8
Scale 1"= 0.8 miles

N

19 Bayview - Muddy Hollow - Laguna

Distance: 4.6 miles   Shaded: 30%
Elevation Change: 600'   Grasses may crowd trail.
Rating: Hiking - 9   Trail can be wet in winter. Some poison oak.
When to Go: Excellent anytime, best in April and May.

This hike descends the slope of Inverness Ridge offering great views to the west, then enters a lush riparian corridor spared by the fire.

0.0 Start at the Bayview trailhead and take Bayview trail west. The hike starts in what was once a mixture of Bishop pine and coastal scrub. Most of the pine burned in the fire of 1995, while the understory of huckleberry, coffeeberry, coyote bush, ferns and blackberry returned quickly. Good views to the ocean.

1.4 The trail drops down into a scenic canyon and riparian corridor dominated by red alder. Nettles, miner's lettuce, sedges and cow parsnip provide a lush, green understory.

In the spring, the succulent leaves and stems of miner's lettuce, also known as Indian lettuce, provided a nourishing treat for Native Americans and early settlers.

Miner's Lettuce

1.6 Junction with Drakes View trail. Continue left. Up ahead, the trail crosses a wooden bridge, then passes through a small marshy area. Farther ahead, majestic old buckeyes, their contorted branches covered with lichen, overhang the trail.

2.1 Junction #1 with the Muddy Hollow road. Head left and watch for birds along the creek and in the marsh.

2.4 Junction with the Limantour Road. Cross the road and continue along the pavement past the Pt. Reyes Youth hostel. Follow the signs to the Laguna trailhead.

2.8 Junction #2 with the Laguna trail. Just past the residence, take the Laguna trail left. Up ahead, the trail enters an open, grassy meadow. The Clem Miller Environmental Center can be seen on the left. A short loop trail up Hidden Valley takes off on the right.

At the end of the meadow, the trail, which was once the main road to the beach, starts a moderate climb up the slopes of Inverness Ridge.

4.1 Junction #3 with the Bayview trail. Head left.

4.6 Bayview trailhead. No facilities.

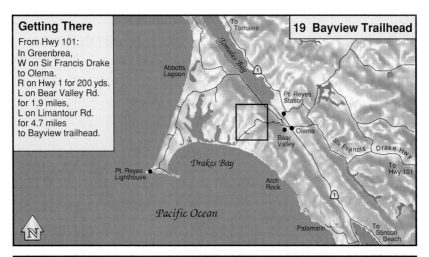

Getting There

From Hwy 101:
In Greenbrea,
W on Sir Francis Drake
to Olema.
R on Hwy 1 for 200 yds.
L on Bear Valley Rd.
for 1.9 miles,
L on Limantour Rd.
for 4.7 miles
to Bayview trailhead.

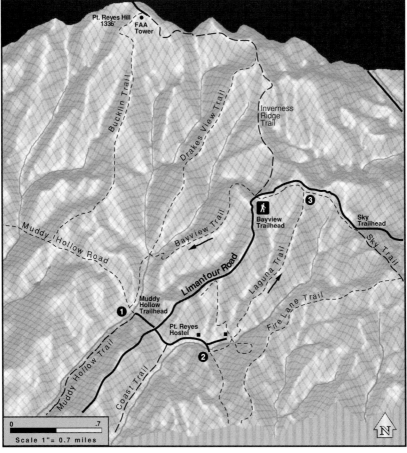

Scale 1"= 0.7 miles

20 Inverness Ridge - Bucklin - Bayview

Distance: 8.4 miles   Shaded: 40%
Elevation Change: 1400'   Moderately steep. Rocky in places.
Rating: Hiking - 8   May be crowded with grasses.
When to Go: Good when clear, best in spring.
This is the best hike for seeing the effects of the 1995 fire on Bishop pine forest along Inverness Ridge. It also offers great views.

0.0 Start at the Bayview trailhead and take the signed Inverness Ridge trail north past the gate and head downhill through coastal scrub and what remains of the Bishop pine forest.

Up ahead, the trail levels out on an open ridgetop covered with dense coastal scrub, an ideal home for brush rabbits.

Small mammals faired poorly in the fire, especially those with burrows. An estimated 95% of the 2000 Point Reyes mountain beaver in the fire zone were believed to have died in their burrows.

Brush Rabbit

1.0 Gate. Go 100 yds. past the gate, up the paved road, to pick up the trail to the left, which now climbs steeply through the burned Bishop pine forest.

1.4 Junction #1. Continue straight to pass through a mix of new Bishop pine seedlings and coastal scrub that includes ceanothus, coyote bush, manzanita, oak, madrone, blackberry, coffeeberry, bracken fern, salal and monkeyflower.

Up ahead, the trail enters a dense stand of dead Bishop pine.

2.1 Good views. After crossing an open saddle, the trail heads steeply uphill through coastal scrub and grasses that occasionally crowd the narrow rutted path. Great views to Tomales Bay.

3.1 FAA Station and junction #2 on Point Reyes Hill at elevation 1336'. Continue along the paved road about 50 yds. to pick up the Bucklin trail which follows the green fence west, then heads downhill. The hike now rolls down a mostly open ridgeline offering great views of Drakes Bay and the headlands. In the spring, look for the white, hairy star tulip.

5.5 Junction #3 with the Muddy Hollow Road. Head left.

6.3 Junction #4 with the Bayview trail. Head left and start the long easy climb towards Inverness Ridge.

8.4 Back at the trailhead. No facilities.

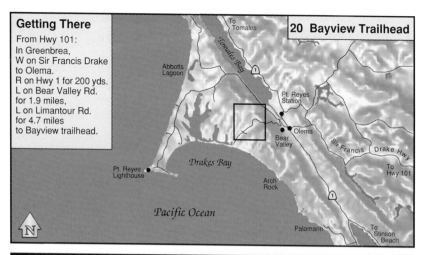

Getting There

From Hwy 101:
In Greenbrea,
W on Sir Francis Drake
to Olema.
R on Hwy 1 for 200 yds.
L on Bear Valley Rd.
for 1.9 miles,
L on Limantour Rd.
for 4.7 miles
to Bayview trailhead.

To Tomales

Tomales Bay

Abbotts Lagoon

Pt. Reyes Station

1

Olema

Bear Valley

Sir Francis Drake Hwy

To Hwy 101

Pt. Reyes Lighthouse

Drakes Bay

Arch Rock

1

Palomarin

To Stinson Beach

Pacific Ocean

N

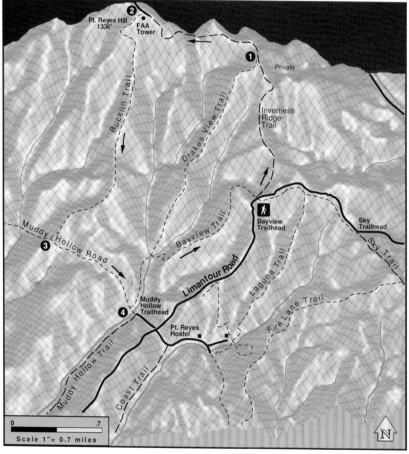

❷

Pt. Reyes Hill 1336'

FAA Tower

❶

Private

Bucklin Trail

Drakes View Trail

Inverness Ridge Trail

❸ Muddy Hollow Road

Bayview Trail

Bayview Trailhead

Sky Trailhead

Limantour Road

Laguna Trail

Sky Trail

❹ Muddy Hollow Trailhead

Pt. Reyes Hostel

Fire Lane Trail

Muddy Hollow Trail

Coast Trail

0 .7
Scale 1"= 0.7 miles

N

21 Coast - Beach - Muddy Hollow Trails

Distance: 4.8 miles   Shaded: 30%
Elevation Change: 200'
Rating: Hiking - 9   Trail may be impassable. See note below.
When to Go: Best in fall and winter for birds.

This hike travels along creeks, fresh and saltwater marshes and the ocean to offer a variety of habitats and good birding locations.

Note: There may be 4-6" of water on the Muddy Hollow trail. In 1995, the creek silted up, causing the creek to meander. Eventually, the park service will rerout the creek or put in a boardwalk.

0.0 Park at the Muddy Hollow parking area 0.2 mile north of the Limantour Road. The hike starts by heading back up toward the road.

0.2 Limantour Road. Continue across the road towards the hostel.

0.4 Junction #1. Before reaching the hostel, take the Coast trail south towards Drakes Bay. The Coast trail parallels a riparian corridor following a small creek into Limantour Marsh. In the early morning, the chatter of birds fills the air.

Brown Pelican

1.3 Creek crossing and alders. Up ahead, the trail skirts the marsh, then doglegs to the right towards the ocean.

2.1 Junction #2 with the beach. Take the signed trail 30' through the dunes and head right along the beach. If it's not too windy, this can be an exhilarating walk with views of Drakes Bay, refreshing ocean breakers and much beach activity. Watch for pelicans, willets and plovers. Keep an eye out for sand crabs and rock louse.

Willet

2.9 Trail inland #3. Look for the greatest concentration of people or a break in the dunes and head inland towards the Limantour parking area. This beach is popular for sunning and wading.

3.0 Junction, water and restroom. At the restroom, head left to pick up the Muddy Hollow trail. Look for sandpipers, willets, egrets and herons in Limantour Estero to the west.

3.4 Junction #4 with the Estero trail. Continue heading inland. The Muddy Hollow trail passes in and out of a riparian community with creeks and marshes lined with red alders.

4.8 Back at the Muddy Hollow parking area. No facilities.

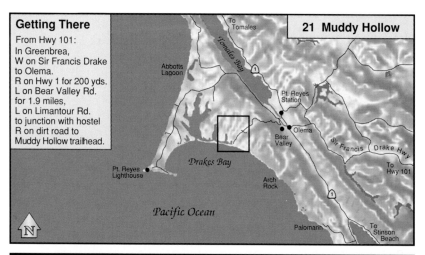

Getting There

From Hwy 101:
In Greenbrea,
W on Sir Francis Drake
to Olema.
R on Hwy 1 for 200 yds.
L on Bear Valley Rd.
for 1.9 miles,
L on Limantour Rd.
to junction with hostel
R on dirt road to
Muddy Hollow trailhead.

To Tomales

Tomales Bay

Abbotts Lagoon

Pt. Reyes Station

Olema

Bear Valley

Sir Francis Drake Hwy

To Hwy 101

Pt. Reyes Lighthouse

Drakes Bay

Arch Rock

Palomarin

To Stinson Beach

Pacific Ocean

N

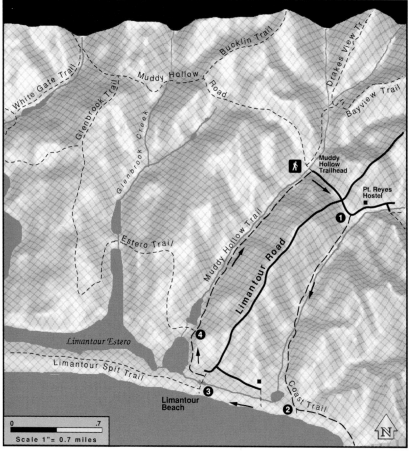

White Gate Trail

Glenbrook Trail

Muddy Hollow Road

Bucklin Trail

Drakes View Tr.

Bayview Trail

Glenbrook Creek

Muddy Hollow Trailhead

Pt. Reyes Hostel

Estero Trail

Muddy Hollow Trail

Limantour Road

1

Limantour Estero

4

Limantour Spit Trail

3

Limantour Beach

Coast Trail

2

0	.7

Scale 1" = 0.7 miles

N

49

22 Muddy Hollow - Estero Trails

Distance: 6.7 miles   Shaded: 20%
Elevation Change: 450'   May be impassable. See note Hike 21.
Rating: Hiking - 7   Poison oak, nettles and mud possible. Windy.
When to Go: Good when clear skies, best in spring, but not too wet.

This hike traverses open coastal hills offering excellent views of Drakes Bay and Limantour Estero, then returns via Muddy Hollow.

0.0 Start at the Muddy Hollow trailhead located 0.2 mile north of Limantour Road. Take the dirt road northeast through the gate.

0.1 Junction. Continue past the Bayview trail and the site of the old Muddy Hollow ranch, which was located near the cypress trees. If the road is wet, look for deer tracks in the wet sandy soil.

0.9 Junction #1 with the Bucklin trail. Continue straight and follow the road as it heads down into the Glenbrook Creek drainage basin.

1.5 Junction #2. Take the Glenbrook trail left and make a short climb to a rise offering great views of the coast. As you start down a long run towards the ocean, the view of Drakes Bay keeps getting better.

2.2 Junction #3 with the Estero trail. Continue towards the ocean.

2.9 Turning point. The trail now reverses direction to head back inland. **Option**: For a side trip, take the unmarked trail 0.1 to 0.4 miles to various views overlooking the estero and Limantour Beach.

3.7 Bridge. As you head inland, the trail drops down past eucalyptus trees. The first dairy on Point Reyes was established here in 1857 by the Steele brothers. Up ahead, the trail crosses a bridge on Glenbrook Creek. This section of trail can be muddy and overgrown with stinging nettles. After crossing the bridge, the trail makes a short climb up to a ridge. On the way, look south to see if you can spot the broken dam where the creek enters Limantour Estero.

5.2 Dam. The last section of Estero trail drops down a muddy, rutted bank to a pond, then crosses a dam that can be overgrown with shrubs. Watch out for poison oak.

5.3 Junction #4 and side trip. Take the Muddy Hollow trail to the left. **Option**: For a side trip, go right 0.4 miles to Limantour Beach.

The Muddy Hollow trail skirts a pond and then a creek that provide good birding. As this ravine has silted up, the creek has meandered, now crossing the trail. Look for lots of new alder trees along the way.

6.7 Back at the Muddy Hollow trailhead. No facilities.

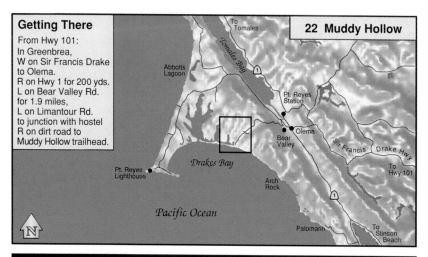

Getting There

From Hwy 101:
In Greenbrea,
W on Sir Francis Drake
to Olema.
R on Hwy 1 for 200 yds.
L on Bear Valley Rd.
for 1.9 miles,
L on Limantour Rd.
to junction with hostel
R on dirt road to
Muddy Hollow trailhead.

22 Muddy Hollow

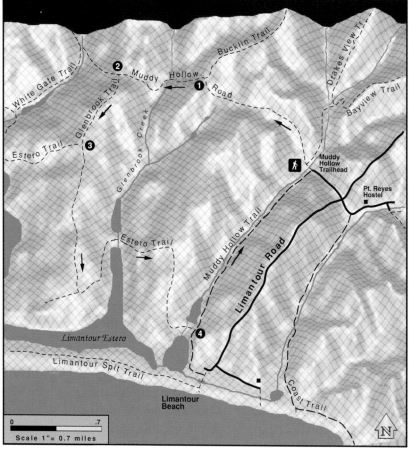

51

23 Limantour Spit - Beach Trails

Distance: 2.0 miles   Shaded: 0%
Elevation Change: less than 100'
Rating: Hiking - 8   Can be very windy.
When to Go: Anytime, best when calm and clear.

This refreshing hike along the dunes and beach provides good views, lots of birds and a reminder of the historic struggle to create a park.

0.0 Start at the Limantour parking area and head down past the restroom towards the ocean. Just after passing the marsh area, turn right and head north along the trail in the dunes.

This trail was once called Limantour Drive, which led into a subdivision called Drakes Bay Estates. This area of the development had been divided into over one hundred lots. When the National Seashore formed in 1962, six of the lots already had homes built! As you walk along, you'll see an occasional pipe or concrete pad, reminders of the heroic efforts of the early conservationists to create a new park.

Modern landowners were not the first to use this spit. Before the developers moved in, archeologists had uncovered three middens, or shell mounds, that were garbage dumps of the Coastal Miwoks. Not only did the middens contain shells, but archeologists also found dozens of pieces of Chinese Ming porcelain and other artifacts that indicate that Cermeno may have camped on the spit after the shipwreck of the San Agustin in 1595.

0.5 Birds of the estero. Look for egrets, herons, willets, and plovers especially in winter.

Harbor Seal

1.0 End of the road. Head out across the dunes to the beach, then go left again. **Option**: To add to the hike, continue northwest 1.8 miles to the end of the spit. (You might see an old shipwreck buried in the sand about 1.5 miles out.)

1.5 Harbor seal or sea lion? The two most common marine mammals at Point Reyes are harbor seals and sea lions. Harbor seals are smaller and have a mottled coat. They have large eyes and no ears. When they go under, they often sink straight down, while sea lions tend to dive forward.

Sea Lion

2.0 Limantour parking area, restrooms and water.

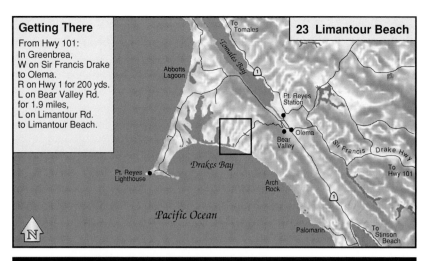

Getting There

From Hwy 101:
In Greenbrea,
W on Sir Francis Drake
to Olema.
R on Hwy 1 for 200 yds.
L on Bear Valley Rd.
for 1.9 miles,
L on Limantour Rd.
to Limantour Beach.

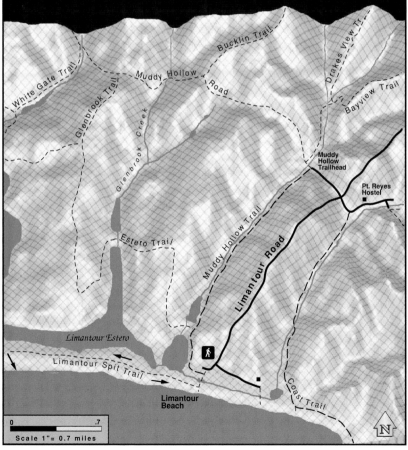

53

24 Beach Trail to Sculptured Beach

Distance: 5.4 miles   Shaded: 0%
Elevation Change: 50'
Rating: Hiking - 7   Check tide tables before taking this hike.
When to Go: Best at low tide in the summer and fall.
This hike explores the interesting rock formations and tidepools on the beaches south of Limantour. Conditions vary with beach level.

0.0 Park in the auxiliary parking area south of the main parking lot at Limantour Beach. Take the trail across the dunes to the beach and head south. Before leaving the dunes, look back and note the trees and ranger residence, which provide a landmark for returning.

1.4 Creek, Coast Camp and junction #1. Continue along the beach.

1.8 Santa Maria Creek and Sculptured Beach. The sandy beach here changes with the seasons. Some winters, large wave action moves sand offshore lowering the level of the beach and making travel over the rocky terraces difficult. In the summer and fall, smaller wave action brings the sand back ashore and it is easier to walk along here and explore the rocks and tidepools.

2.5 Junction #2. You can climb up to a small rocky terrace and scan the beach south to Pt. Resistance. Usually, this is as far as you can go. When done exploring, retrace your steps or take the stairs up to return via the Coast trail.

Option: If the beach sand level is high enough and there is a minus tide, you may be able to explore the beach south. You will probably have to climb down off the terrace 4-6 feet to reach the beach. If you can safely do this, there are interesting caves and tunnels ahead. (This is not an approved park trail. Hike at your own risk and be sure to watch the tide!)

Low Tide

Low tide at Point Reyes occurs 30-40 minutes earlier than Golden Gate low tide, which is usually given in the tide tables.

Also, the tide comes in slowly at first, then rises more quickly about two hours after the minimum. You should plan to have a clear, safe route off any beach by this time.

3.6 Junction #1 and Coast Camp. Head inland, veer left and follow the Coast trail north.

4.8 Junction #3. Leave the Coast trail and take the beach north.

5.3 Junction. Look for the trees and residence and head inland again.

5.4 Parking area. Restrooms and water at the main parking area.

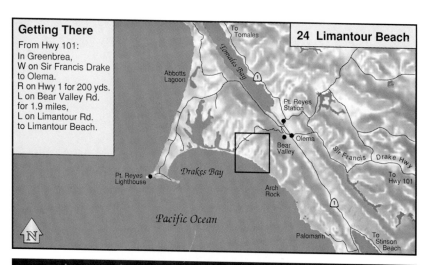

Getting There

From Hwy 101:
In Greenbrea,
W on Sir Francis Drake
to Olema.
R on Hwy 1 for 200 yds.
L on Bear Valley Rd.
for 1.9 miles,
L on Limantour Rd.
to Limantour Beach.

To Tomales

Tomales Bay

Abbotts Lagoon

Pt. Reyes Station

Olema

Bear Valley

Sir Francis Drake Hwy

To Hwy 101

Pt. Reyes Lighthouse

Drakes Bay

Arch Rock

Palomarin

To Stinson Beach

Pacific Ocean

N

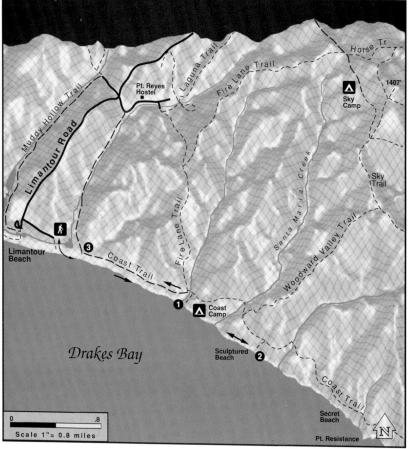

Horse Tr

Laguna Trail

Fire Lane Trail

Pt. Reyes Hostel

Muddy Hollow Trail

1407'

Sky Camp

Sky Trail

Limantour Road

Santa Maria Creek

Woodward Valley Trail

Limantour Beach

3

Coast Trail

Fire Lane Trail

1

Coast Camp

Sculptured Beach

2

Drakes Bay

Coast Trail

Secret Beach

Pt. Resistance

N

Scale 1"= 0.8 miles

0   .8

25 PR Lighthouse and Chimney Rock

Distance: 1.2, 0.4 and 1.6 miles   Shaded: 0%
Elevation Change: 400' for lighthouse   Wind and fog likely.
Rating: Hiking - 10   Check weather at 415-663-9029.
When to Go: Best in early January and again in March-April.

These are three exhilarating hikes. The lighthouse offers whale watching. Chimney Rock has elephant seals and great wildflowers.

Note: During peak visitor times, usually December to April, the park service restricts traffic to the lighthouse and Chimney Rock, and runs a bus shuttle from the South Beach parking lot during the hours from 10 am to 2 pm. Call the above number for information.

To the PR Lighthouse and Back – 1.2 miles and 400' Change.

0.0 Start at the lighthouse parking lot and head uphill past the gate. The view north along Point Reyes Beach, which runs 11 miles, offers a classic picture-taking spot.

0.5 Visitor Center. The center is open Thursday to Monday, 10 am to 5 pm. The lighthouse stairs, all 308 of them, are open from 10 am to 4:30 pm Th-M, weather permitting. Check the Visitor Center for tours of the lighthouse itself. The lighthouse platform is the best place in Marin to watch grey whales migrating from Alaska to Baja California.

To Elephant Seal Overlook and Back – 0.4 miles and 50' Change

0.0 From the Chimney Rock trailhead, head downhill on the paved road 50' and pick up the trail heading towards Drakes Beach.

0.2 Overlook. Usually, docents are available to describe elephant seal mating and breeding habits. Spotting scopes may be set up.

To Chimney Rock and Back – 1.6 miles and 100' Change.

0.0 From the Chimney Rock trailhead, follow the trail as it skirts the hillside above the cypress trees and ranger residence.

0.3 Junction with Underhill road. Continue straight. The US Coast Guard Lifeboat Station, below, operated between 1927 and 1968. Dozens of people were saved after shipwrecks near here.

0.4 Junction #1. Take the Overlook trail to the right.

0.5 Overlook and views. Towering 500' cliffs provide spectacular coastline scenery. Head back, then right towards Chimney Rock.

0.9 Chimney Rock and wildflowers. Expert observers have counted over 60 species of flowers along the trail including hairy cat's-ears, Johnny-tuck, paintbrush, lupine, iris and checkerbloom.

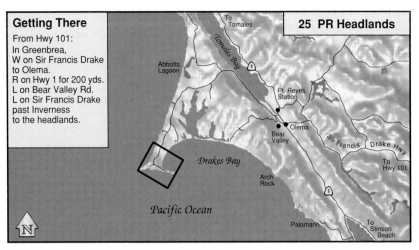

Getting There

From Hwy 101:
In Greenbrea,
W on Sir Francis Drake
to Olema.
R on Hwy 1 for 200 yds.
L on Bear Valley Rd.
L on Sir Francis Drake
past Inverness
to the headlands.

25 PR Headlands

To
Tomales

Abbotts
Lagoon

Tomales Bay

1

Pt. Reyes
Station

Olema

Bear
Valley

Sir Francis Drake Hwy

To
Hwy 101

Drakes Bay

Arch
Rock

1

Pacific Ocean

Palomarin

To
Stinson
Beach

N

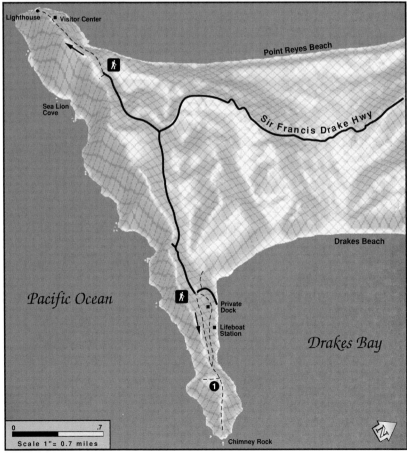

Lighthouse   Visitor Center

Point Reyes Beach

Sea Lion
Cove

Sir Francis Drake Hwy

Drakes Beach

Pacific Ocean

Private
Dock

Lifeboat
Station

Drakes Bay

1

0   .7

Scale 1"= 0.7 miles

Chimney Rock

26 Drakes Beach Trail

Distance: 2.5 miles   Shaded: 0%
Elevation Change: 300'   Some parts may not be passable.
Rating: Hiking - 9   Creek crossing required.
When to Go: Best at low tide, good wildflowers in April and May.

This hike explores the beach and historic marker commemorating Drake's landing. It then climbs inland for views and flowers.

0.0 Start at the Ken Patrick Visitor Center picnic area and take the trail left on to the beach. As you walk along the beach and terraces, see if you can spot fault lines in the cliff above. These show up as shifts in the horizontal lines.

These light-colored cliffs reminded Drake of the "white cliffs of Dover" and are strong evidence that Drake beached his ship here. He named this land, Nova Albion, meaning New England.

0.5 Horseshoe Pond and Dam. **Note:** Be sure to go up towards the dam and look carefully at the road coming down the hill slightly to your left. This is your return route. Check the creek level connecting the road to the beach. If this looks too difficult, you should return via the beach. Also, check the hillside for cows or bulls. See note below.

0.6 Beach. If the tide is not too high, continue down the beach past the cliffs and dunes to the estero.

1.2 Drakes Estero. If possible, circle the dunes and head towards the cliff and trees.

1.3 Drake's Memorial. Look for the pole and monument about 50' inland. Most experts believe that this is the spot where Drake careened the Golden Hinde for repairs in 1579.

One of two monuments to Sir Francis Drake at Drakes Beach.

Note: The hike continues through the gate and up the road into pasture. If you are concerned about cows or bulls, then return via the beach. However, the pasture has great wildflowers in spring.

1.8 Horseshoe Pond. Look for a creek crossing. Do not go up on the bluff for a crossing. It is unsafe.

2.5 Back at the Visitor Center with restrooms and snack bar.

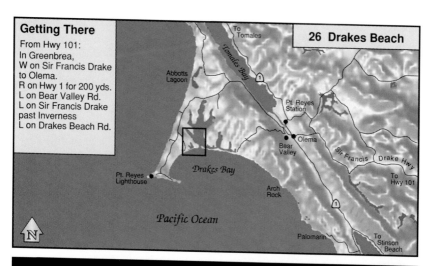

Getting There

From Hwy 101:
In Greenbrea,
W on Sir Francis Drake
to Olema.
R on Hwy 1 for 200 yds.
L on Bear Valley Rd.
L on Sir Francis Drake
past Inverness
L on Drakes Beach Rd.

26 Drakes Beach

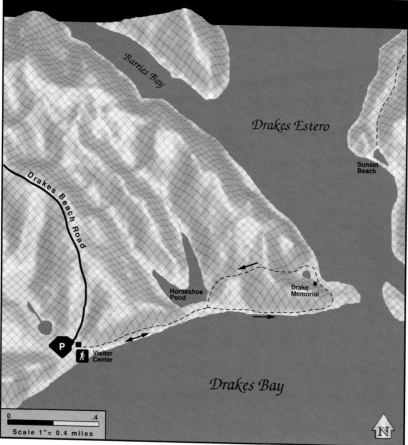

59

27 Estero - Drakes Head Trails

Distance: 9.4 miles   Shaded: 0%
Elevation Change: 750'
Rating: Hiking - 8   Trail can be muddy in parts.
When to Go: Best in late fall and winter when calm and clear.

This is an out and back hike through rolling pasture to the best viewpoint on Point Reyes. A good hike to see birds and mammals.

0.0 Start at the parking area off the paved road. Go through the fence and follow the Estero trail south towards the pine forest. This rangeland is part of Home Ranch which has been grazed since the 1850s. In spring, patches of deep-blue iris dot the hillsides.

1.1 Dam and bridge at point #1. Crossing the bridge of Home Bay, notice the Home Ranch farm buildings to the east. James Shafter's ranch, started in 1857, is the oldest surviving ranch on Point Reyes.

The trail now heads uphill past lupine and coyote bush. Watch for wildlife along the way - deer, rabbits, osprey, ducks and egrets.

1.6 Plateau and view of Drakes Estero. The point across the water was one of several schooner
landing sites. The estero and bay were deeper in earlier days allowing small schooners, like the *Point Reyes*, to deliver highly-prized butter to San Francisco.

Johnson's Oyster Farm now uses the shallower estero waters.

2.6 Junction #2 with the Sunset Beach trail. Bear left, head uphill.

Schooner Point Reyes

3.3 Junction #3 and corral. Turn right and follow the signed Drakes Head trail towards the ocean.

4.2 Water tank and trees. This is the site of the Drakes Head Ranch, which operated from the 1850s to 1960. Keep to the right.

4.7 Drakes Head. On a clear day this is the best view spot on all of Point Reyes! (Caution: The cliff edge may be unstable.) It offers a panoramic sweep of Drakes Bay from the headlands to Double Point. Look for harbor seals sunning at the end of the spit. When you are ready to return, retrace your steps.

9.4 Back at the parking lot. Restrooms available.

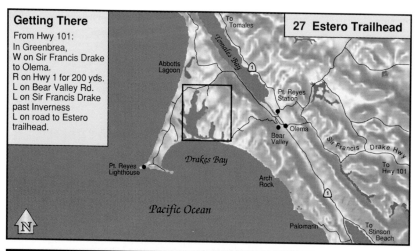

Getting There

From Hwy 101:
In Greenbrea,
W on Sir Francis Drake
to Olema.
R on Hwy 1 for 200 yds.
L on Bear Valley Rd.
L on Sir Francis Drake
past Inverness
L on road to Estero
trailhead.

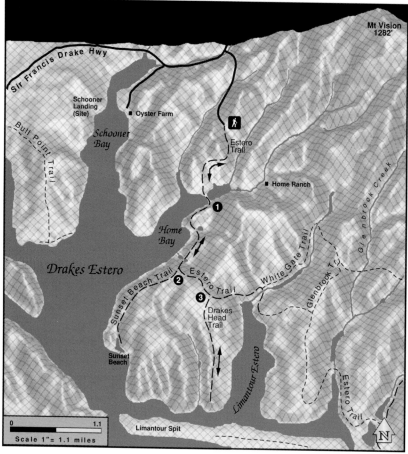

28 Bull Point and South Beach Trails

Distance: 4.0 and 2.0 miles   Shaded: 0%
Elevation Change: 100'   Can be very windy.
Rating: Hiking - 6   May be bulls in pasture.
When to Go: In spring to Bull Point. Fall and winter on the beach.

One hike leads through flowers and pasture to a great view of Drakes Estero, while the other hike explores the ocean beach.

Bull Point Trail – 4.0 miles and 150' Change

0.0 Park at the signed Bull Point trailhead just past the AT&T antenna farm on Sir Francis Drake Hwy. The hike passes through a fence and follows an old ranch road towards Drakes Estero. The large group of Cypress trees to the north was the site of F Ranch established in 1852. It also housed the first post office on Point Reyes in a small room off the kitchen.

0.8 Spring and moist area. A spring on the left provides water for cows and moisture for the tall evergreen shrub, wax myrtle. On the right, notice the pilings at the end of Creamery Bay. This was one of several schooner landings on Point Reyes that was used to deliver dairy products to San Francisco and bring supplies to the ranches.

1.9 Estero and junction #1. The trail ends at a cliff overlooking the estero. You can continue 250 yds. left for access to the beach and more views of Drakes Estero or go 100 yds. to the right for beach access and a driftwood bench.

South Beach Trail – 2.0 miles and 0' Change

Note: Dangerous surf! Do not swim or wade in the ocean.

0.0 Park at the end of the South Beach parking lot. The hike starts by heading south along the beach with views towards the Point Reyes Headlands. The lighthouse light can be

*Life Saving Station
Operated from 1890-1927*

seen flashing at the edge of the cliff, but the lighthouse itself can not be seen. Lots of driftwood washes ashore at this end of the beach.

1.0 Coast Guard Life-Saving Station. The buildings (which are private) on the cliff were part of the life-saving station that later moved to Drakes Bay. At least 38 shipwrecks occurred at Point Reyes.

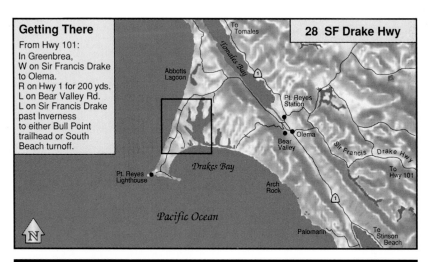

Getting There

From Hwy 101:
In Greenbrea,
W on Sir Francis Drake
to Olema.
R on Hwy 1 for 200 yds.
L on Bear Valley Rd.
L on Sir Francis Drake
past Inverness
to either Bull Point
trailhead or South
Beach turnoff.

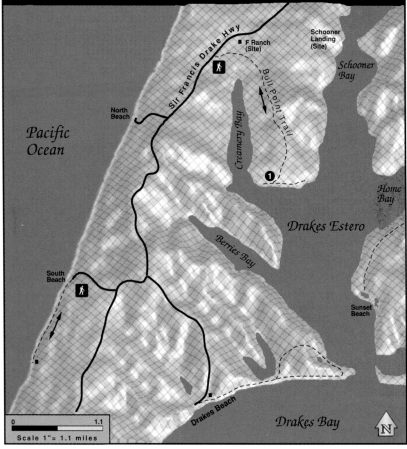

Scale 1"= 1.1 miles

63

29 Johnstone - Jepson Trails

Distance: 4.5 miles   Shaded: 80%
Elevation Change: 500'
Rating: Hiking - 10   Can be muddy in winter.
When to Go: Great anytime. Birds in winter, wading in summer.
This is a magnificent hike through Tomales Bay State Park. It features a luxuriant Bishop pine forest, Indian Nature trail and three beaches.

Option: If you want to picnic or wade in the bay after the hike, you might drive into the park (pay fee) and start the hike at mile 2.1 below.

0.0 Start at the small parking area located one mile out Pierce Point Rd. and two-tenths of a mile before the entrance to Tomales Bay State Park. Take the signed Jepson trail uphill into Bishop pine forest.

0.1 Junction. Head right towards signed Shell Beach.

0.3 Junction #1. Take the Johnstone trail left towards Pebble Beach. Up ahead, after crossing the road again, the trail enters a luxuriant forest produced by winter rain and summer fog drip.

1.6 Junction #2. Continue right past the restroom to delightful Pebble Beach. When ready to continue, return to junction #2 and take the trail towards Heart's Desire Beach. Up ahead, toyon and huckleberry shrubs are almost twice their normal size in this lush rainforest.

2.0 Junction. A trail leads left to the parking circle. Continue straight towards Heart's Desire. Great views of the bay.

2.1 Heart's Desire Beach. Continue across the beach, past the restroom and take the signed Indian Nature trail to Indian Beach.

2.3 Junction #3 with the Loop trail. Keep to the right.

2.6 Bridge and Indian Beach. Head down the beach towards the Indian kotchas. The hike continues on the road that circles the marsh.

3.2 Junction. Leave the road and take the loop trail left.

3.3 Junction #3 again. Head right.

3.5 Heart's Desire Beach. Cross the beach and take the Johnstone trail along the shoreline.

3.6 Junction. Head right up to the parking lot, then circle around counterclockwise on the paved street.

3.7 Junction. Take the signed Jepson trail uphill.

4.4 Junction with the trail to Shell Beach. Stay right.

4.5 Back at the parking area. No facilities.

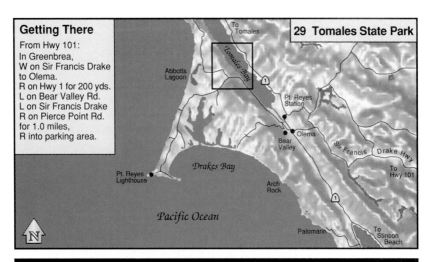

Getting There

From Hwy 101:
In Greenbrea,
W on Sir Francis Drake
to Olema.
R on Hwy 1 for 200 yds.
L on Bear Valley Rd.
L on Sir Francis Drake
R on Pierce Point Rd.
for 1.0 miles,
R into parking area.

To Tomales

Tomales Bay

Abbotts Lagoon

Pt. Reyes Station

Olema

Bear Valley

Sir Francis Drake Hwy

To Hwy 101

Pt. Reyes Lighthouse

Drakes Bay

Arch Rock

Pacific Ocean

Palomarin

To Stinson Beach

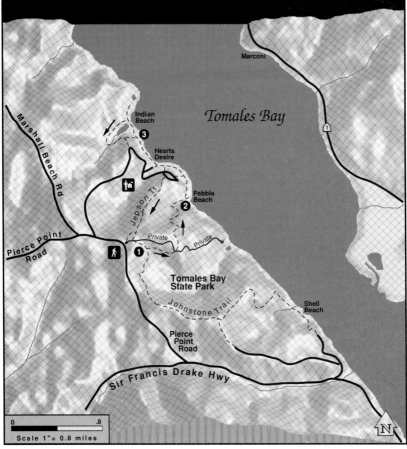

Marconi

Indian Beach

Tomales Bay

Hearts Desire

Marshall Beach Rd

Jepson Tr.

Pebble Beach

Private

Private

Pierce Point Road

Tomales Bay State Park

Johnstone Trail

Shell Beach

Pierce Point Road

Sir Francis Drake Hwy

Scale 1"= 0.8 miles

30 Abbotts Lagoon and Ocean Beaches

Distance: 3.0, 1.2 and 0.8 miles   Shaded: 0%
Elevation Change: 100' to 300'
Rating: Hiking - 8   Kehoe Beach trail can be wet.
When to Go: Best weather in fall and winter, best flowers in spring.

All three of these trails provide access to ocean beaches on the northern end of Point Reyes. Good birding at Abbotts Lagoon.

Note: Dangerous Surf! Do not swim or wade in the ocean here.

Abbotts Lagoon Trail – 3.0 miles and 100' Change

0.0 Start at the trailhead located 3.4 miles along the Pierce Point Road and head west across the open pasture. In the spring of wet years, these fields are aglow with yellow poppies and fiddleneck.

1.1 Bridge, lagoon, wildflowers and birds. Yellow goldfields cover the hill on the left, while the bridge offers a good view spot for shore birds. Cross the bridge and follow the edge of the lagoon to the ocean.

1.5 Point Reyes Beach is also called Ten-mile Beach and Great Beach. This beach is a nesting area for the snowy plover. From April to June, you may see hatching enclosures that protect the plovers nest from predators, mainly crows that eat the eggs. These enclosures have increased chick survival rates from 3% to 60%.

Kehoe Beach Trail – 1.2 miles and 100' Change

0.0 Start at the trailhead 5.5 miles along the Pierce Point Road. This is a level trail that parallels Kehoe Marsh out to the beach. Good birding in the winter and abundant wildflowers in the spring.

0.6 Beach and wildflowers. The cliffs on the right are often covered in goldfields, poppies, lupine and baby blue eyes in April and May. There are good tidepools to the far right during very low tides.

McClures Beach Trail – 0.8 miles and 300' Change (See map 32)

0.0 The trailhead is located at the end of the Pierce Point Road, 9.5 miles from the Sir Francis Drake Hwy. junction. The trail follows a ravine as it descends 300' to the ocean.

On the way down, notice the occasional erosion on the hillside. This is caused by herds of tule elk that range at this end of Tomales Point.

0.4 Beach. This is the most picturesque of the ocean beaches. During super-low tides, there are great tidepools at the south end of the beach. Be sure to check the tide tables and plan your return while the tide is still low.

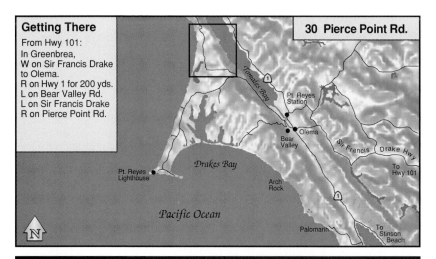

Getting There

From Hwy 101:
In Greenbrea,
W on Sir Francis Drake
to Olema.
R on Hwy 1 for 200 yds.
L on Bear Valley Rd.
L on Sir Francis Drake
R on Pierce Point Rd.

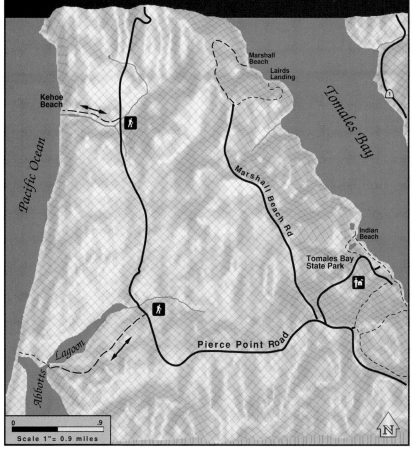

67

31 Marshall Beach and Lairds Landing

Distance: 2.4 and 2.6 miles   Shaded: 10%
Elevation Change: 360' for both
Rating: Hiking - 8   Can be windy at the start.
When to Go: Best weather in fall and winter, best flowers in spring.

These two hikes start at the same place and take different routes to Tomales Bay. Both offer great views of the bay and a little history.

Note: At tides below +1.0', it is possible to get from Marshall Beach to Lairds Landing by walking along a rocky beach, thus combining the two hikes into a loop trip. However, the rocks are slippery and the 200 yd. trip requires a small amount of climbing. Low tide occurs here about one hour later than times given in the tidebook.

Lairds Landing Trail – 2.4 miles and 360' Change

0.0 From the Marshall Beach parking area, head east through the gate and down the paved road. Along the way, you find tremendous views north to Marshall Beach and east across Tomales Bay.

1.2 At Lairds Landing, you may find several interesting old structures where artist Clayton Lewis lived from the 1960s until he died in 1995. One of the buildings is very small and seems like a cross between a doll house and a guest cottage. Most of these buildings are scheduled for removal. When the buildings are removed, interpretive

Marshall Beach as seen from the trail to Lairds Landing

signs will be put up to describe the history of the site.

Marshall Beach Trail – 2.6 miles and 360' Change

0.0 From the Marshall Beach parking area, head north and take the trail through pasture, then down towards a cypress grove. In the spring, look for a small white calochortus, called hairy pussy ears.

1.2 Cove and beach. This picturesque beach offers sunbathing, picnicking, wading and views across Tomales Bay to the town of Marshall. In 1875, Marshall was a stop on the North Pacific Coast Railroad. It was also the site of the West Coast's first wireless communications system. Today, it houses oyster farms and Tomales Bay's only remaining boatyard.

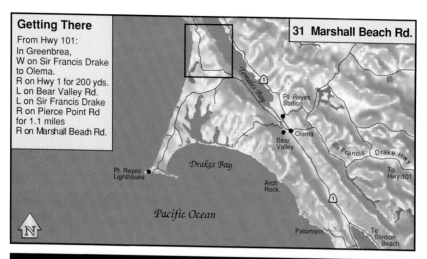

Getting There

From Hwy 101:
In Greenbrea,
W on Sir Francis Drake
to Olema.
R on Hwy 1 for 200 yds.
L on Bear Valley Rd.
L on Sir Francis Drake
R on Pierce Point Rd
for 1.1 miles
R on Marshall Beach Rd.

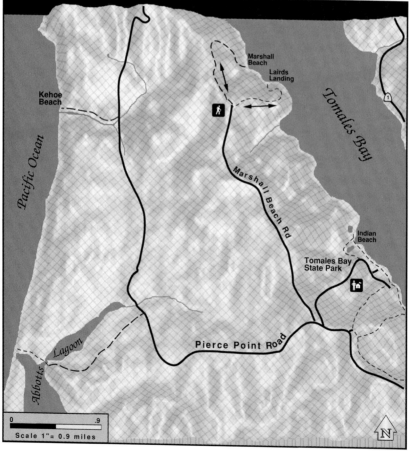

69

32 Tomales Point Trail

Distance: 9.4 miles   Shaded: 0%
Elevation Change: 1000'
Rating: Hiking - 9   Can be very windy and/or foggy.
When to Go: Winter is good; best flowers in April and May.
This hike along an open, exposed ridge can be spectacular or miserable depending on the weather. Carry ponchos in case of fog.

0.0 Start at the parking lot at the end of Pierce Point Road. Follow the signs around the old dairy ranch. If fog cuts your hike short, you can tour the ranch when you get back.

0.8 Point #1 with spectacular coastal views. Just before the trail turns inland, you can see the dramatic coastal cliffs to the north rising over 400' above the ocean. In spring, this spot also provides a great wildflower display with yellow gold fields, tidy tips, buttercups, sun cups, poppies, lupine and wild strawberries.

1.0 The trail heads inland offering a view east down White Gulch to Hog Island in Tomales Bay.

Watch for Tule elk and for their large V-shaped tracks on the trail.

2.5 Highest point at 471'. As you climb to the highest spot on Pierce Point, you can see across Bodega Bay to the Bodega headlands and the Sonoma coast. On clear days, look for the jutting profile of Mt. Saint Helena 30 miles northeast.

Tule Elk

3.3 Lower Pierce Ranch site and unmarked junction #2. At the ravine, near the cypress trees, a small trail heads right down the right side of the ravine to a beach on Tomales Bay. Continue on the main trail.

4.0 Bird Rock viewpoint. If the tide is right, you can see a blowhole on the left side of the rock. From here, the trail climbs through a sandy area and dunes.

4.7 Tomales Point. In 1852, the English merchant ship, *Oxford*, mistaking Tomales Bay for San Francisco Bay, came full sail into the bay until she ran permanently aground just before Hog Island. After enjoying the view, retrace your steps back south.

9.4 Back at Pierce Point trailhead. Restrooms available.

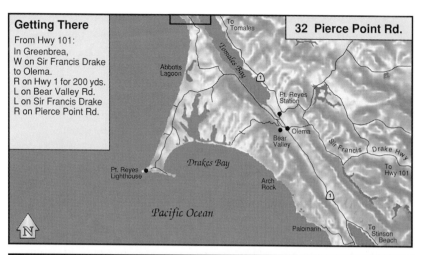

Getting There

From Hwy 101:
In Greenbrea,
W on Sir Francis Drake
to Olema.
R on Hwy 1 for 200 yds.
L on Bear Valley Rd.
L on Sir Francis Drake
R on Pierce Point Rd.

To Tomales

Abbotis Lagoon

Pt. Reyes Station

Olema

Bear Valley

Sir Francis Drake Hwy

To Hwy 101

Pt. Reyes Lighthouse

Drakes Bay

Arch Rock

Pacific Ocean

Palomarin

To Stinson Beach

N

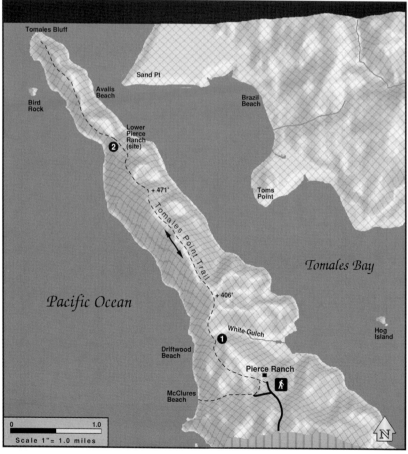

Tomales Bluff

Sand Pt

Avalis Beach

Bird Rock

Brazil Beach

Lower Pierce Ranch (site)

❷

+ 471'

Toms Point

Tomales Point Trail

Tomales Bay

Pacific Ocean

+ 406'

White Gulch

❶

Hog Island

Driftwood Beach

Pierce Ranch

🚶

McClures Beach

0   1.0

Scale 1"= 1.0 miles

N

33 Five Brooks Trailhead to Bear Valley*

Distance: 4.4 miles   Shaded: 70%
Elevation Change: 200'   Lots of horse traffic possible.
Rating: Hiking - 7   Can be muddy in winter, dusty in summer.
When to Go: Best in winter and spring, but not when real wet.

This one-way hike explores the terrain of the San Andreas rift zone. Vegetation includes forest, meadow, pasture and wildflowers.

*Shuttle Hike. Leave pickup cars at Bear Valley and shuttle all hikers to the Five Brooks parking area and trailhead.

0.0 Go through the gate and head west towards Inverness Ridge.

0.1 Junction. Continue past the Rift Zone trail.

0.2 Junction #1. Take the Stewart trail right towards the north.

0.3 Junction. Go through the metal gate and head downhill. California hazelnut dominates the understory here. At the bottom of the hill, continue straight past the restroom to the edge of a meadow and the Stewart horse camp, then head left to cross the creek.

0.4 Creek. At the creek, take the signed Rift Zone trail left.

1.4 Private property. A sign indicates that the trail is now crossing land owned by the Vedanta Society, a religious retreat organization.

2.9 Junction #2. Go through the gate, head right 100' and then left across the pasture. Up ahead, look for a glimpse of the Vedanta retreat house about one-half mile on your left. This magnificent old Victorian, called "The Oaks", was solidly built out of redwood by James Shafter in 1869 and easily survived the 1906 earthquake. James Shafter, and his brother, Oscar, two lawyers from Vermont, at one time owned most of the Point Reyes peninsula.

The Oaks ca. 1920s

3.8 Road. The hike passes through a gate and crosses the main road to the Vedanta house. The area before the gates can be muddy if cows have churned up the soil. After passing through the second gate, the trail skirts a seasonal marsh, climbs a knoll, then drops into a meadow leading to Bear Valley.

4.4 Bear Valley trailhead with full facilities.

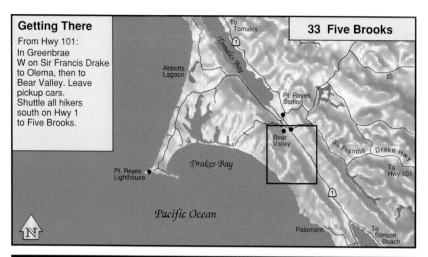

Getting There

From Hwy 101:
In Greenbrae
W on Sir Francis Drake
to Olema, then to
Bear Valley. Leave
pickup cars.
Shuttle all hikers
south on Hwy 1
to Five Brooks.

33 Five Brooks

To Tomales

Tomales Bay

Abbotts
Lagoon

Pt. Reyes
Station

Bear
Valley

Sir Francis   Drake Hwy

To
Hwy 101

Pt. Reyes
Lighthouse

Drakes Bay

Pacific Ocean

Palomarin

To
Stinson
Beach

N

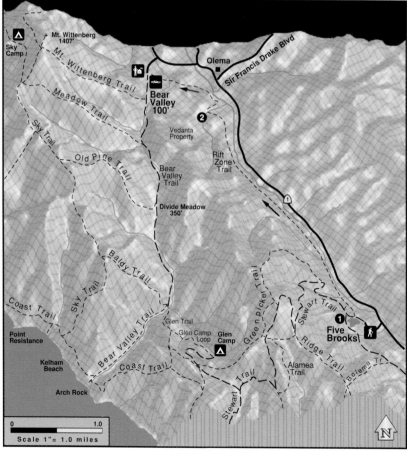

Sky
Camp

Mt. Wittenberg
1407'

Mt. Wittenberg Trail

Olema

Sir Francis Drake Blvd

Bear
Valley
100'

Meadow Trail

Vedanta
Property

Sky Trail

Old Pine Trail

Bear
Valley
Trail

Rift
Zone
Trail

Divide Meadow
350'

Baldy Trail

Sky Trail

Coast Trail

Bear Valley Trail

Glen Trail

Green picker Trail

Stewart Trail

Five
Brooks

Point
Resistance

Glen Camp
Loop

Glen
Camp

Ridge Trail

Bolema Trl.

Kelham
Beach

Coast Trail

Stewart Trail

Alamea
Trail

Arch Rock

0   1.0

Scale 1"= 1.0 miles

N

73

34 Kehoe Beach to Abbotts Lagoon*

Distance: 4.6 miles   Shaded: 0%
Elevation Change: 100'   Trail can be wet near the marsh.
Rating: Hiking - 7   Includes 2 miles on beach.
When to Go: Best in April and May when not too windy.

This one-way trail and beach hike is one of the three best wildflower hikes on Point Reyes. Go in the morning before winds get too strong.

*Shuttle Hike. Leave pickup cars at Abbotts Lagoon trailhead, 3.4 miles along the Pierce Point Road and shuttle hikers another 2.1 miles to the Kehoe Beach trailhead.

0.0 The trail starts next to an exposed slab of Monterey shale on the northern hillside and follows a mostly level path through sandy soil to the beach. On the left, Kehoe Marsh provides freshwater habitat for sedges, reeds and birds. In spring, the grassy hills on the right are dotted with fragrant bush lupine and occasional patches of iris.

0.5 Dunes, cliffs and wildflowers. Take the narrow path towards the right along the exposed cliff to view gold fields, poppies, tidy tips, baby blue eyes and blue lupine.

At the beach, head down by the water and hike along the wet sand south towards Abbotts Lagoon.

3.1 Abbotts Lagoon. You should be able to spot the lagoon from the beach by looking for a low-lying opening in the dunes. The lagoon is close to the ocean

Gold Fields

and low enough in elevation that heavy breakers enter it at high tide to create brackish water. Follow the northern edge of the lagoon inland. Look for the yellow flowers of lizard tail along the way.

3.5 Bridge and wildflowers. Cross the bridge and enjoy another hillside covered in gold. Just like Chimney Rock and Kehoe Beach, the best wildflower displays often appear in the most hostile environments. Up ahead, notice the wind-pruned coastal scrub on the hillside opposite the lagoon. Also, keep an eye out for birds.

Continue following the trail as it heads inland to the east. After crossing a small swale, the trail passes through fields of poppies, lupine, mustard and orange fiddleneck.

4.6 Abbotts Lagoon trailhead with pickup cars and restrooms.

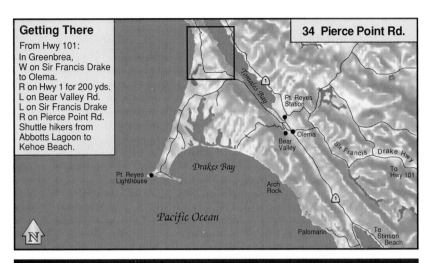

Getting There

From Hwy 101:
In Greenbrea,
W on Sir Francis Drake
to Olema.
R on Hwy 1 for 200 yds.
L on Bear Valley Rd.
L on Sir Francis Drake
R on Pierce Point Rd.
Shuttle hikers from
Abbotts Lagoon to
Kehoe Beach.

34 Pierce Point Rd.

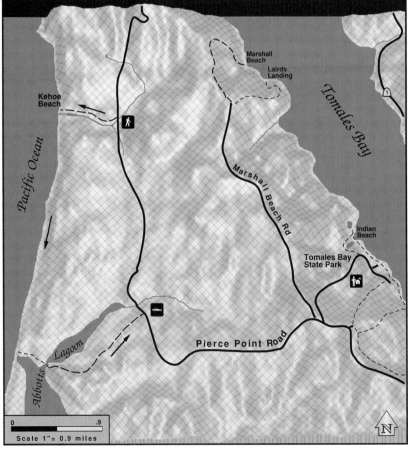

75

35 Olema Valley to Five Brooks*

Distance: 5.5 miles   Shaded: 30%
Elevation Change: 600'   Moderately steep.
Rating: Hiking - 8   Trail can be impassable. Poison oak.
When to Go: Excellent anytime, best when the hills are green.
This one-way hike meanders, like the local creeks, through a mixture
of vegetation along the San Andreas fault zone.

*Shuttle Hike. Leave pickup cars at Five Brooks and shuttle all hikers
to the Olema Valley trailhead at mile marker 18.17, north of Dogtown.

Note: The trail passes through a marshy area that can have 1-3" of
standing water in winter and spring. Also, there are many deep holes
along the trail created by horses' hooves sinking into soft mud. Within
the first mile, the trail crosses two creeks that can be 3-6" deep during
wet weather (more if raining). Rocks can make the crossing easier.

0.0 The trail starts in a meadow and heads northwest with good
views to Inverness Ridge to the west.

0.4 Junction #1 with the Teixeira trail. Continue north through the
marsh area, past grasses and tall, poison hemlock.

0.8 Creek crossings. The trail crosses Pine Gulch Creek, which
follows an old faultline on its way to Bolinas Lagoon.

1.6 Earthquake country. Rolling hills, sag ponds, small scarps
(slides) and slumps provide topographic evidence of the thousands of
earthquakes that have formed the Olema Valley rift zone.

This variety of terrain supports a variety of vegetation. Alders line the
creeks. Douglas fir and bay trees compete for light along the moist
hillsides. Meadows, dotted with coyote bush and coffeeberry, offer
open views to the surrounding hills.

2.7 Junction #2 with a spur trail to the highway and the Randall trail.
Continue north. If the trail is damp, look for animal tracks.

4.0 Junction #3 with the Bolema trail. This is the highest point on the
hike at 700'. Bear right and start a moderately steep descent through
dense cover of Douglas fir with ferns, hazelnut, vines and nettles.

4.8 Small bridge. Up ahead, the creek widens into a broad, flat
streambed shaded by a thicket of alders and bays.

5.2 Junction. The trail right heads to the stables. Continue left.

5.3 Junction #4. Bear right to skirt the lake back to the trailhead.

5.5 Five Brooks trailhead. Pickup cars, tables, water and restrooms.

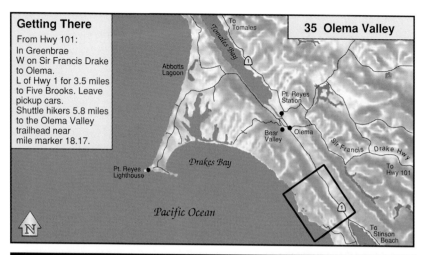

Getting There

From Hwy 101:
In Greenbrae
W on Sir Francis Drake
to Olema.
L of Hwy 1 for 3.5 miles
to Five Brooks. Leave
pickup cars.
Shuttle hikers 5.8 miles
to the Olema Valley
trailhead near
mile marker 18.17.

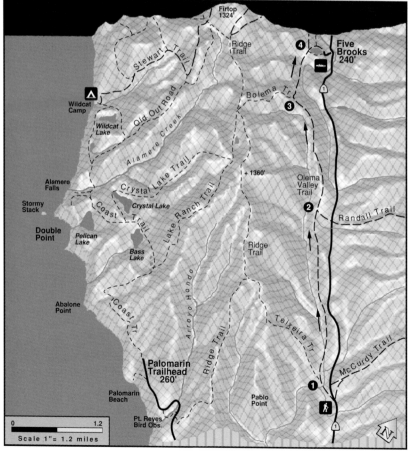

77

36 Pierce Point Road to Shell Beach*

Distance: 5.7 miles   Shaded: 90%
Elevation Change: 1100' down, 600' up.   Poison oak possible.
Rating: Hiking - 9   Beaches crowded in summer.
When to Go: Great anytime. Best early fall for swimming and berries.

This one-way hike in Tomales Bay State Park makes a loop down to Heart's Desire Beach, then heads towards Shell Beach.

*Shuttle Hike. Leave pickup cars in the parking area in Tomales Bay State Park at the end of Camino Del Mar. Shuttle all hikers to the small parking area located one mile out Pierce Point Rd.

0.0 Take the signed Jepson trail uphill into Bishop pine forest.

0.1 Junction. Head left towards signed Heart's Desire
Beach. Ahead, the trail enters the Jepson Memorial
Grove, one of the finest groves of Bishop pine in
California. Bishop pine are smaller than most pines.
They have two needles per bunch, each about 3"
long. Cones are tightly bound to branches.

Bishop Pine

Option: You can cut the hike short by 2.5 miles and save 500' of climbing by heading right towards Shell Beach (switch to jct #3 below).

0.8 Parking lot. Head left around the parking circle to find the trail.

0.9 Junction #1 with the Johnstone trail. Head left.

1.0 Heart's Desire Beach. Return to junction #1.

1.1 Continue on the signed Johnstone trail towards Pebble Beach.

1.5 Junction #2. Head left past the restroom to
Pebble Beach. Return here to continue the hike
towards Shell Beach.

2.8 Junction #3. Head left on the Johnstone trail to
Shell Beach. Down below, the trail crosses the
upper end of a lush ravine.

Huckleberry

3.3 Bench and viewpoint. Good views east to Tomales
Bay. Caution: Poison oak crowds the trail, but is sometimes difficult to spot. Up ahead, look for ripe huckleberries in the fall.

3.9 Junction #4. Continue left to start a long gradual descent.

5.4 Shell Beach and restroom. This small sandy beach offers good picnicking and swimming. Continue the hike across the beach.

5.7 Beach. Continue across the beach to the parking area and cars.

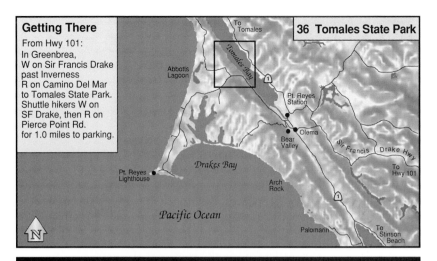

Getting There

From Hwy 101:
In Greenbrea,
W on Sir Francis Drake
past Inverness
R on Camino Del Mar
to Tomales State Park.
Shuttle hikers W on
SF Drake, then R on
Pierce Point Rd.
for 1.0 miles to parking.

36 Tomales State Park

To
Tomales

Tomales Bay

Abbotts
Lagoon

1

Pt. Reyes
Station

Olema
Bear
Valley

Sir Francis Drake Hwy

To
Hwy 101

Pt. Reyes
Lighthouse

Drakes Bay

Arch
Rock

1

Palomarin

To
Stinson
Beach

Pacific Ocean

N

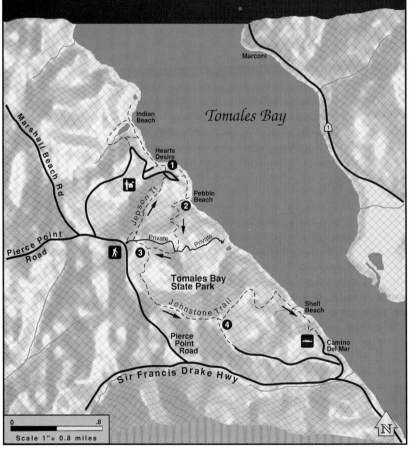

Marconi

Tomales Bay

Indian
Beach

Marshall Beach Rd

Hearts
Desire
1

Jepson Tr

Pebble
Beach
2

Pierce Point
Road

Private

Private

3

Tomales Bay
State Park

Johnstone Trail

4

Shell
Beach

Camino
Del Mar

Pierce
Point
Road

Sir Francis Drake Hwy

1

0   .8

Scale 1"= 0.8 miles

N

79

37 Sky Trailhead to Bear Valley*

Distance: 7.3 miles   Shaded: 70%
Elevation Change: 750' up and 1300' down
Rating: Hiking - 10
When to Go: Excellent anytime, best when clear.
This is the easiest and best all-around hike for exploring the forested Inverness Ridge and Bear Valley. Good views too.

*Shuttle Hike. Leave pickup cars at Bear Valley and shuttle all hikers to the Sky trailhead about 3.5 miles along the Limantour Road.

0.0 The Sky trail starts by heading south up an old ranch road.

0.8 Junction #1. Take the Horse trail left through dense vegetation along the moist, north-facing slope of Mt. Wittenberg. Up ahead, the trail circles a landslide that occurred in 1982.

1.2 Junction. Turn right and head uphill on the Z Ranch trail.

1.9 Junction #2. The grassy slopes of Mt. Wittenberg and Sky Camp below provide a picturesque foreground to Drakes Bay and the Point Reyes headlands. Take the summit trail left up to the top.

2.1 Mt. Wittenberg at 1407' is the highest spot on Point Reyes. Lots of young fir trees dot the hillside, so enjoy the views while they last. Retrace your steps down the mountain when ready to continue.

2.3 Junction. Take the Mt. Wittenberg trail south along the ridge line.

2.7 Two junctions. Continue south on the Sky trail, which now enters a magnificent forest of Douglas fir towering over a smaller forest of elderberry. In early spring, the light-green leaves of the elderberry provide a striking contrast to the darker colors of the fir. Later in spring, cream-colored blossoms and inedible red berries create changing patterns in this woodsy setting.

Red Elderberry

3.5 Junction #3 with the Woodward Valley trail. Continue straight.

3.8 Junction #4. Take the Old Pine trail left as it leaves the Inverness Ridge and makes a long, gradual descent down to Bear Valley. Before you go, notice that a few trees were singed by the fire. Fire fighters made a stand here and kept the fire from burning the ridge.

5.7 Junction #5 and Divide Meadow. Head downhill to the left.

7.3 Bear Valley trailhead with water, restrooms and pickup cars.

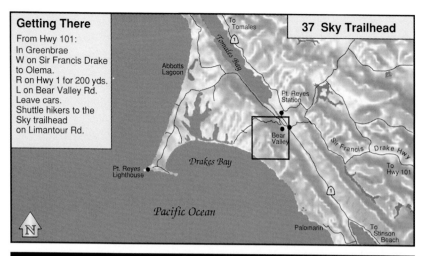

Getting There

From Hwy 101:
In Greenbrae
W on Sir Francis Drake
to Olema.
R on Hwy 1 for 200 yds.
L on Bear Valley Rd.
Leave cars.
Shuttle hikers to the
Sky trailhead
on Limantour Rd.

37 Sky Trailhead

To
Tomales

Tomales Bay

Abbotts
Lagoon

Pt. Reyes
Station

Bear
Valley

Sir Francis   Drake Hwy

To
Hwy 101

Drakes Bay

Pt. Reyes
Lighthouse

Palomarin

To
Stinson
Beach

Pacific Ocean

N

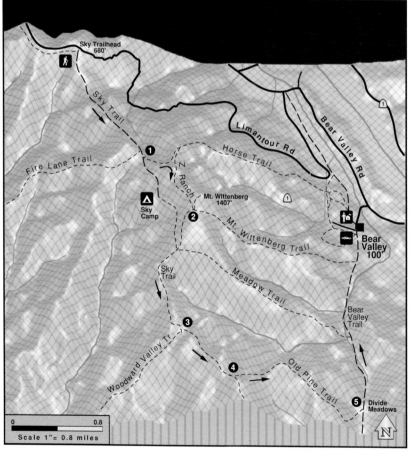

Sky Trailhead
680'

Sky Trail

Fire Lane Trail

Limantour Rd

Bear Valley Rd

Horse Trail

1

N Ranch

Sky
Camp

Mt. Wittenberg
1407'

2

Mt. Wittenberg Trail

Sky
Trail

Meadow Trail

Bear
Valley
100'

Bear
Valley
Trail

3

Woodward Valley Tr.

4

Old Pine Trail

5 Divide
Meadows

0   0.8

Scale 1"= 0.8 miles

N

A1 A Selection of Best Trails

Not sure where to go? Here is our selection of best trails. Remember that the season and weather strongly influence trail conditions.

The 3 Best Beginner Trails
1. Bear Valley trail, Hike 4
2. Bear Valley and Inverness Ridge trails, Hike 3
3. Bear Valley Interpretive trails, Hike 1

The 3 Best Wildflower Trails
1. Chimney Rock, Hike 25
2. Kehoe Beach and Abbotts Lagoon trails, Hike 30
3. Either Tomales Pt., Hike 32 or the Coast trail, Hikes 6 and 15

The 3 Best Creek and Waterfall Trails
1. Bear Valley, Hike 4
2. Alamere Falls, an extension of Hike 13
3. Fern Canyon Nature trail at PRBO, Hike 12

The 3 Best View Trails
1. Drakes Head, Hike 27
2. Double Point, Hike 13
3. Either Chimney Rock, Hike 25 or the Coast trail, Hikes 6 and 7

The 3 Best Birding Areas
1. Abbotts Lagoon, Hike 30
2. Muddy Hollow, Hikes 21 and 22
3. Limantour Estero, Hike 23

The 3 Best Flora Trails
1. Bear Valley, Hikes 2, 3, and 4
2. Inverness Ridge, Hikes 6 and 7
3. Greenpicker trail, Hikes 9 and 10

The 3 Best Beach Trails
1. Drakes Beach, Hike 26
2. Limantour Beach, Hike 24
3. Sculptured Beach, Hike 23 (low tide only)

The 3 Best Foggy Day Trails
1. Bear Valley, Hike 4
2. Olema Valley and Inverness Ridge, Hike 8
3. Bear Valley and Inverness Ridge, Hike 3

A2 A Trail for All Seasons

December – January

The sun is at its lowest angle of the year and it's often cold and wet. But now you can discover one of the great secrets of Point Reyes. Head for the coast where it can be warm and sunny, especially during foggy days inland. Now is also the time for whale and seal watching, and for discovering migrating waterfowl. Hikes 12, 13, 14 and 21 through 32 are all good choices.

February – March

This is great hiking time. Water runoff is high. The whales are heading north and elephant seal pups learn to swim. Milkmaids, hound's tongue and Douglas iris start the wildflower parade. If the coast is clear, go there first, especially the south-facing areas. Otherwise head inland. Good hikes include 4, 7, 13, 14, 15, 25, 26 and 27.

April – May

This is the premier hiking time of the year. The hills are gloriously green and wildflowers are peaking. If it's not foggy or windy, be sure to try one of the coastal wildflower areas, either Tomales Point, Chimney Rock, Drakes Head or Abbotts Lagoon. All of the hikes are great, especially Hikes 6, 15, 25, 26, 27, 30, 32 and 34.

June – July

While summer fog can make the coast cold and miserable, fog drip on the Inverness Ridge can provide a welcome relief to the hot interior. Some summer wildflowers, monkeyflower, poppy, yarrow and clarkia, hang on while the hills turn brown. Hikes 3, 8, 9, 10, 20, 29 and 36.

August – September

Now is the time to avoid the dry, dusty roads. Let the weather be your guide. Try the coast first, then the ridges. Head for north-facing trails, creeks, conifer forests and ripe huckleberries. Hikes 4, 5, 14, 19, 21, 22, 29, 30, 31, and 32.

October – November

Look for fall colors from poison oak, big leaf maple and California black oak. First winter storms can mean gusty winds, clear days and marvelous views. It's a good time for coastal trails, beaches and tidepools. Hikes 4, 12, 21, 23, 24, 26, 30, 31 and 32.

A3 Backpacking Camps

There are four backcamping camps at Point Reyes. These campgrounds are free of charge. However, a camping permit is required. Permits are available at the Visitor Center and reservations for them can be made up to two months in advance. Reservations are almost always necessary for summer, holidays and weekends - phone 415-663-1092.

All camp sites have water (check first), restrooms, tables and charcoal grills. No wood gathering is allowed. All campgrounds have metal poles for hanging food packs. There are no bears, but raccoons are plentiful. There is very little shade at any of the camps, so be prepared for sun, wind or fog.

The safest overnight parking is at the Visitor Center at Bear Valley. However, do not leave valuables in the car anywhere. All of the camps are accessible by bicycle on designated trails.

Sky Camp

Sky Camp has 12 sites and is located on the grassy slopes of Mt. Wittenberg, 1020' above sea level. It has the most secluded individual camp sites and offers the best views, especially of Drakes Bay and the headlands.

The shortest route to Sky Camp is 1.2 miles starting from the Sky trailhead, see Hike 18. The best medium distance hike from Bear Valley is via the Old Pine trail, a distance of 5.4 miles along Hike 3.

The bicycle route to Sky Camp starts from the Sky trailhead, Hike 18.

Coast Camp

Coast Camp has 14 sites and is located just south of Limantour Beach at an elevation of 100'. It offers easy access to Sculptured Beach (pick up a tide book at the Visitor Center). Some sites are exposed to strong northwest winds.

The shortest route to Coast Camp is 1.5 miles from Limantour Beach, see Hike 24. The best route from Bear Valley lies along the Old Pine and Woodward Valley trails, 6.7 miles. Start out on Hike 3, then switch over to Hike 6 at the Woodward Valley junction.

The bike route starts from the Muddy Hollow area, see Hike 22.

Glen Camp

Glen Camp has 12 sites and is located in a small meadow at an elevation of 600'. It is the most isolated and secluded of the four backpacking camps and some sites are shaded.

The best route to Glen Camp starts from Bear Valley and is 4.6 miles along Hike 7. If you want more climbing, you can start from Five Brooks and hike the Stewart trail over Firtop at 1324', then take the Greenpicker trail for a total distance of 5.0 miles, see Hike 9.

The bicycle route to Glen Camp is along the Stewart trail to the Glen trail, then the Glen Camp Loop trail, start on Hike 9.

Wildcat Camp

Wildcat Camp has 12 sites and is located in an open grassy meadow just above Wildcat Beach. It offers easy access to the beach and Alamere Falls. It is about two miles from Double Point.

The easist route to Wildcat Camp is to hike 5.5 miles north along the Coast trail from Palomarin, see Hike 15. From Bear Valley, you can start on Hike 7 and hike a total of 6.3 miles to Wildcat Camp. You can also reach the camp from Five Brooks by starting out on Hike 9 and hiking a total distance of 5.7 miles.

The bicycle route follows the Stewart trail, see Hike 9.

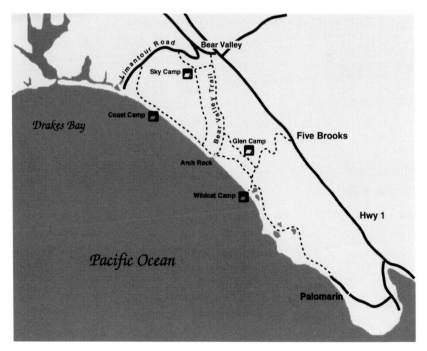

McClures Beach

McClures Beach is the most scenic of the north section beaches. It is a sandy beach, almost a mile long, with large granite cliffs blocking the ends. It is a great beach for picnicking and watching waves.

At low tide, you can climb through a slot in the cliffs at the south end of the beach to explore a smaller beach and tidepools.

Kehoe Beach

Kehoe Beach is at the north end of a long beach with three names: Great Beach, Ten-Mile Beach or Point Reyes Beach. At low tide, you can explore the beach north. There are good tidepools past the rocky area, which is slippery and difficult to cross.

Abbotts Lagoon

Abbotts Lagoon is known for its winter birds, spring wildflowers, summer winds and fall canoeing. Canoes should be portaged about 1/2 mile from a road location just north of the main parking area.

Point Reyes Beaches, North and South

These two sandy beaches are in the middle of the Great Beach. They are easily accessible with parking located just 100 yds. away. These beaches have abundant driftwood and are great for long walks.

Chimney Rock

This rocky beach has good tidepools. You can access the beach near the Rescue Station, then head southwest towards the ocean. The best tidepools are located past the second prominence, which can only be reached at low tide.

Drakes Bay

This is the best all-around beach at Point Reyes. Its orientation protects it from large ocean waves and the tall cliffs provide some shelter from summer winds. The beach is great for walking, picnicking and wading. The Visitor Center has a small aquarium and exhibits. The Visitor Center and cafe are open daily.

Marshall Beach, Hearts Desire and Shell Beaches

These beaches are located on Tomales Bay where both air and water temperature are warmer. Swimming is possible. Hearts Desire and Shell Beaches are in Tomales Bay State Park and are more crowded.

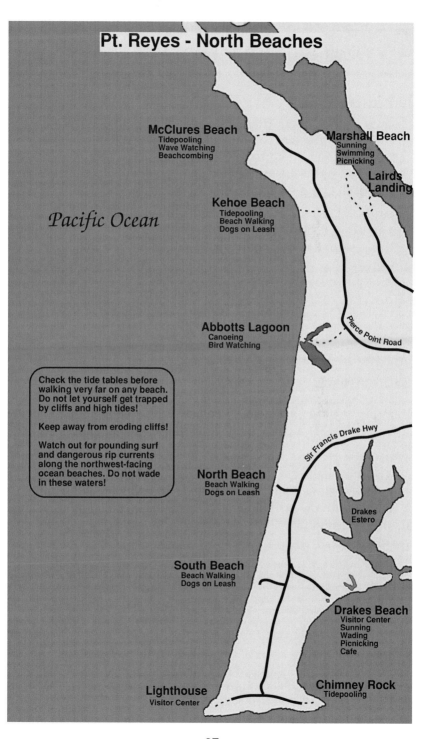

Pt. Reyes - North Beaches

Pacific Ocean

McClures Beach
Tidepooling
Wave Watching
Beachcombing

Marshall Beach
Sunning
Swimming
Picnicking

Lairds Landing

Kehoe Beach
Tidepooling
Beach Walking
Dogs on Leash

Abbotts Lagoon
Canoeing
Bird Watching

Pierce Point Road

Check the tide tables before
walking very far on any beach.
Do not let yourself get trapped
by cliffs and high tides!

Keep away from eroding cliffs!

Watch out for pounding surf
and dangerous rip currents
along the northwest-facing
ocean beaches. Do not wade
in these waters!

Sir Francis Drake Hwy

North Beach
Beach Walking
Dogs on Leash

Drakes
Estero

South Beach
Beach Walking
Dogs on Leash

Drakes Beach
Visitor Center
Sunning
Wading
Picnicking
Cafe

Lighthouse
Visitor Center

Chimney Rock
Tidepooling

A5 Southern Beaches

Limantour Beach

Limantour Beach is very popular for picnicking, wading and walking. If you walk towards the north end, look for remains of a shipwreck in the sand about 1/2 mile from the spit. The nearby estero and marshes are good for bird watching.

Sculptured Beach

This is one of the most interesting beaches on Point Reyes. It is best explored at low tide when the sedimentary layers of the marine terrace are exposed.

Sculptured Beach may change as moving sand varies the relationship of the sandy beach to the rocks. At times, usually in the winter, the sand is low, making the beach almost impassable. In the summer and fall, the sand is higher and you can almost stroll along until you reach a small promontory, where you have to climb down 4-6 feet to continue. If you can get past this point, the beach becomes even more interesting with caves, tunnels and tidepools.

Secret Beach

Of all the beaches on this map, Secret Beach is the most difficult one to reach. You can only access it at minus tide and low surf. Even then, it may involve some significant climbing and wading. The only route is past Sculptured Beach (as described above).

Secret Beach itself is a sandy beach about one mile long, ending at Pt. Resistance. Do not plan to stay on Secret Beach for long. You need to return during low tide.

Kelham Beach

This small sandy beach lies between Pt. Resistance and Arch Rock. At very low tide, you can explore the sea tunnel under Arch Rock.

Wildcat Beach

This is a sandy beach two miles long with Alamere Falls at one end. The beach can easily be walked except during high tide. However, you do have to hike at least four miles to get there.

Palomarin Beach

Palomarin Beach is mostly a rocky beach with some marine terraces that can be explored at low tide.

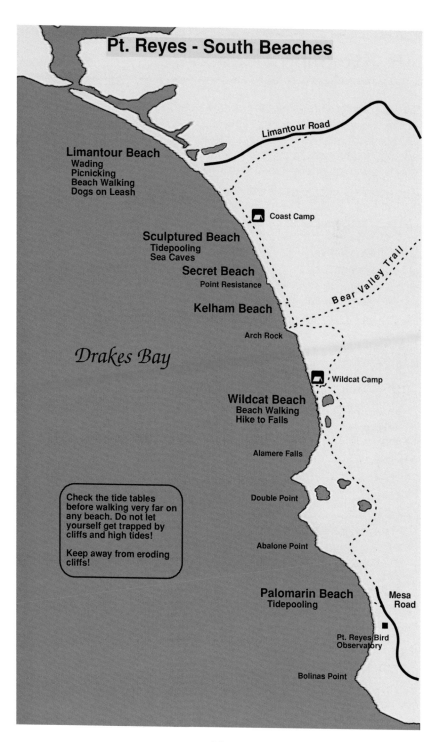

Pt. Reyes - South Beaches

Limantour Road

Limantour Beach
Wading
Picnicking
Beach Walking
Dogs on Leash

Coast Camp

Sculptured Beach
Tidepooling
Sea Caves

Secret Beach
Point Resistance

Bear Valley Trail

Kelham Beach

Arch Rock

Drakes Bay

Wildcat Camp

Wildcat Beach
Beach Walking
Hike to Falls

Alamere Falls

Check the tide tables
before walking very far on
any beach. Do not let
yourself get trapped by
cliffs and high tides!

Keep away from eroding
cliffs!

Double Point

Abalone Point

Palomarin Beach
Tidepooling

Mesa
Road

Pt. Reyes Bird
Observatory

Bolinas Point

A6 Exploring Tidepools

There are two high tides and two low tides daily. The organisms living in the rocky intertidal world between ocean and land are exposed to incredible conditions, crashing waves, flying predators, hot sun and constantly changing temperatures and salinity. Yet, this world is often teeming with invertebrates, organisms that have no backbone.

The intertidal habitat can be divided into four zones as shown below.

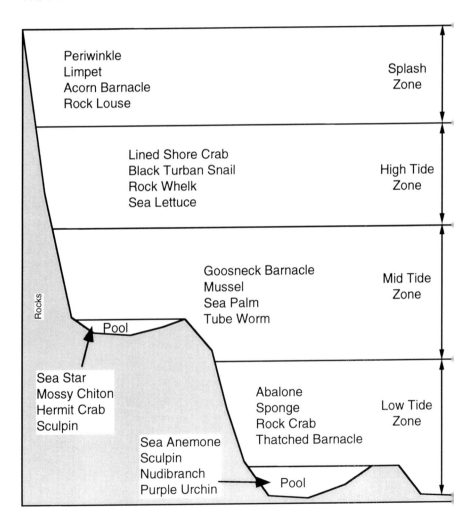

Periwinkle
Limpet
Acorn Barnacle
Rock Louse

Splash Zone

Lined Shore Crab
Black Turban Snail
Rock Whelk
Sea Lettuce

High Tide Zone

Rocks

Pool

Goosneck Barnacle
Mussel
Sea Palm
Tube Worm

Mid Tide Zone

Sea Star
Mossy Chiton
Hermit Crab
Sculpin

Abalone
Sponge
Rock Crab
Thatched Barnacle

Low Tide Zone

Sea Anemone
Sculpin
Nudibranch
Purple Urchin

Pool

Guidelines for exploring tidepools.

- Check the tide tables and plan your trip accordingly.
- Beaches are often windy. Dress with warm layers.
- Tidepool rocks are slippery. Wear tennis shoes or rubber boots.
- Bring a change of clothes in case you get wet.
- The lower you get, the more you'll see.
- Check under rocks, but always replace them like you found them.
- If you pick a critter up, put it back in the same place.
* Keep one eye on the ocean, looking for extra large waves.

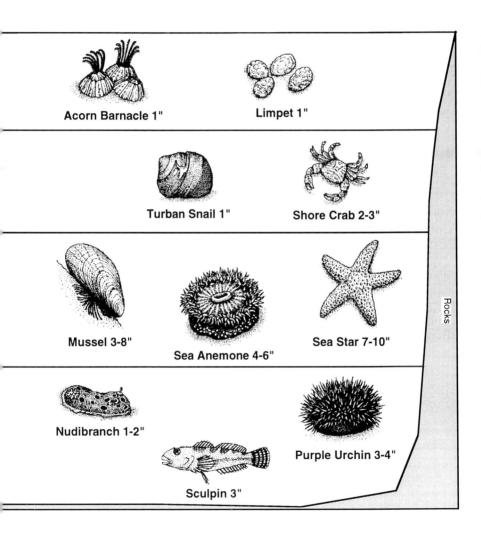

Acorn Barnacle 1"

Limpet 1"

Turban Snail 1"

Shore Crab 2-3"

Mussel 3-8"

Sea Anemone 4-6"

Sea Star 7-10"

Rocks

Nudibranch 1-2"

Sculpin 3"

Purple Urchin 3-4"

A7 Whales and Whalewatching

Each winter, more than 15,000 California grey whales pass Point Reyes on their 6000 mile journey southward to breed in the warm lagoons of Baja California. These whales hug the coastline, often passing within one-quarter mile of the Point Reyes lighthouse and other coastal prominences.

When to Watch

The southward migration of the grey whale begins at Point Reyes in December and peaks in early January. Pregnant females are generally the first to arrive, followed by courtship groups (often two males and one female) and then the adolescents.

The northerly return trip begins passing Point Reyes in early March and is led by newly pregnant females. Newborn young and their mothers arrive later, usually between April and June. They often travel slowly and very close to shore, sometimes entering Drakes Bay, providing a memorable view.

The California Grey Whale

Grey whales almost became extinct during the early 1900s. Their migration and breeding habits made them easy targets for Russian, Japanese and American whaling ships. Fortunately, with protection established along the west coast in 1946, they have made a remarkable comeback.

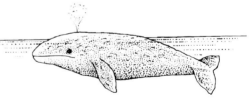

The California grey whale is a baleen whale with rows of long fingernail-like plates (baleen) in the roof of its mouth. These plates are used to filter krill, plankton and other

California Grey Whale

crustaceans from the rich Arctic waters, where they do most of their feeding. One researcher reported that a young female in captivity consumed over 1800 pounds of squid a day, gaining weight at the rate of 2 pounds per hour. Adult males can reach a length of 50 feet and weigh over 30 tons. A new born calf enters the world about the size of a compact car, weighing up to a ton.

Baleen whales have two blowholes in their head where they spout water 10 - 15 feet high. The spout is the most conspicuous sign of the grey whale and lasts from 5-10 seconds. Following the spout, you can often see the tail fluke as the whale heads down for a dive of 20 seconds to 2 minutes.

Where To Go

The Point Reyes lighthouse, 240 feet above the ocean, is the best place to see migrating whales. However, even though the lighthouse is well above sea level, it is still 300 steps below the clifftop. These stairs are open from 10am to 4pm, Thursday through Monday, weather permitting. A small Visitor Center sits atop the bluff, 0.4 miles from the parking area. You can check on whale activity in the Visitor Center before you make the trek down the steps. However, the historic lighthouse itself is well worth a look. Check for the times of ranger-led tours.

During peak months, usually January and February, between 10am and 2pm, the park service restricts traffic to the lighthouse and provides parking and a shuttle bus at the North Beach parking area, three miles away.

Although the lighthouse is only about 20 miles from the main Visitor Center at Bear Valley, it takes about 45 minutes driving time.

Point Reyes Lighthouse

What To Bring

Ideally, the weather will be sunny and calm and you'll see half a dozen whales per hour. However, you can't count on either condition. Bring warm clothing in case of fog and wind. Also, binoculars are essential. Wide-angle binoculars are best, so you can spot whales quickly. Telescopes don't work well because of narrow fields of view.

Other Places to See Whales

Other viewpoints for whalewatching include Double Point (see Hike 13), the Coast trail above Miller Point (see Hike 6) and the Coast trail just north of Palomarin (see Hike 13 or 15).

Other Whales

Two other species of whales that might be seen along the coast include the blue and the humpback whales. Blue whales are the largest creatures on earth, about twice the size of the grey whale and are occasionally seen from May to September. Humpback whales are sometimes seen in August or September.

A8 Elephant Seals and Sea Lions

There are three major populations of pinnipeds that inhabit the waters around Point Reyes, the northern elephant seal, the California sea lion and the harbor seal. Other pinnipeds, including the northern sea lion and the northern fur seal, can also be found at Point Reyes, but their populations are not large.

Northern Elephant Seal

Northern Elephant Seal

During the 1800s, elephant seals were slaughtered for their oil to the brink of extinction. It is believed that a population of about 100 seals survived near Baja California. Both Mexico and the United States gave the elephant seals protected status in the 1920s and the population has made a remarkable recovery to about 160,000 seals along the Pacific Coast.

The elephant seals first returned to Point Reyes in 1981 when a colony was established in a small cove between the lighthouse and Chimney Rock. By 1996, the population was about 1000 seals and growing at the rate of 30% annually. They have expanded to establish new colonies on Point Reyes Beach and on Drakes Beach.

The young adults are the first to arrive, usually in late November or December. Later, they leave when the mature bulls arrive and stage violent battles to establish dominance. In January, the breeding females (cows) arrive to form harems and to give birth to pups. Usually one pup is born to each cow and she nurses the pup for about four weeks. During this time, the pup will grow from 75 pounds at birth to 250-350 pounds. Some resourceful pups nurse from two or three cows and can weigh up to 600 pounds. They are called superweaners.

Caution

It is illegal to disturb breeding seals and sea lions. Please keep at least 100 yds. distance.

When the weaned pups are 4-6 weeks old, they molt and replace their black fur coat with a shiny new silver one. Soon after, the pups learn to swim and leave the colony in April.

Male elephant seals approach maturity at five years, but don't reach their prime breeding years until they are 9-12 years old. Males can weigh as much as 8,000 pounds and be up to 20' in length. Older males develop a large overhanging snout. The "alpha" bull is the dominant bull and does most of the mating in a harem.

Females are much smaller than males, averaging 10-12' in length and weighing 1200-2000 pounds. Females come into season about 25 days after giving birth and may mate several times before returning to the ocean. However, the fertilized egg does not implant in the wall of her uterus for about four months, most likely to give the female time to regain her strength.

When the breeding season is over in April, the females and returning juveniles molt. Elephant seals, like dogs, cats and other mammals, must replace old skin and hair. However, elephant seals do it all at once, rather than year round. In May and June, the young males return to molt and in July and August, the adult males molt.

California Sea Lion

California sea lions are familiar figures along parts of the Pacific Coast. Adult male sea lions grow to 8' and weigh 600 pounds, while females weigh only 200 pounds. Sea lions have articulated flippers that let them "walk" on land and climb rocks.

California Sea Lion

The largest population of sea lions at Point Reyes is usually found in the winter at Sea Lion Cove, which can be seen from an overlook along the road near the lighthouse.

Harbor Seal

Harbor seals are the smallest of the three pinnipeds described with adult males growing to 5' and weighing 250 pounds. There are an estimated 2500 harbor seals along Point Reyes, the largest concentration in California. Harbor seals, like all earless seals, can not bend their hind flippers and are awkward on land.

Harbor seals are often found hauled out along mud flats and sandy beaches like Double Point and Drakes Estero. Numbers increase during the breeding/molting season from April-July. The seals are easily disturbed and will leave the beach at the first sign of danger, which can reduce breeding effectiveness.

A9 Animals and Animal Tracks

Imagine a land abundant with grizzly and black bears, mountain lions, tule elk, deer and coyotes. All evidence suggests that Point Reyes was rich in wild life when Drake landed in 1578. Now, the bears are gone, incompatible with humans and cattle. The coyotes may be returning. Possibly, one or two mountain lions remain and the tule elk, once extinct, are again thriving. The only large mammal to continuously inhabit the land is the mule deer.

Tule Elk

Tule Elk

It is estimated that most of the Tule elk vanished by the 1850s, victims of hunters. The elk were reintroduced in 1978 and are confined to 2600 acres along the northern end of the Point Reyes peninsula. Usually the herd of 300 or more animals is split into four or five smaller herds. The best way to see them is to hike the Tomales Point trail, Hike 32.

Deer

Point Reyes has three species of deer, one native and two introduced. The black-tailed

Mule Deer

or mule deer are native. They are the smallest of the three species and can be identified easily by their black tail and white rump.

The two non-native deer are the axis deer and fallow deer, both brought to Point Reyes in the 1940s by a sport hunter who got them from the San Francisco Zoo. Fallow deer, native to the Mediterranean region, can be identified by their palmated antlers and variable color, which ranges from white to almost black. Males begin rutting in fall and often engage in vigorous conflict. Antlers are shed in the spring.

Axis deer, native to India and the largest of the three species, are best identified by

Fallow Deer

96

their brown coloring with spotted sides. Male antlers are shed in the summer and regrown each fall. Older bucks carry an eye guard or tine near the antler base. Axis deer are often seen in the open headlands north of Limantour road. They are more wary than the others and keep their distance.

Axis Deer

Both species of non-native deer must be culled to keep their numbers down. Park rangers hunt them each winter in order to maintain a population of around 300 deer.

Smaller Animals

There are dozens of smaller animals living on Point Reyes. Jules Evens, *The Natural History of the Point Reyes Peninsula*, lists over 45 species including possums, shrews, moles, bats, beavers and rats. There are two skunks on Point Reyes, the striped and the spotted skunk. Raccoons are plentiful as campers will attest. Three of the more interesting animals are shown here.

Grey Fox

The grey fox is found in coastal scrub, chaparral and grasslands. It sometimes has a reddish hue on its front flanks and can be best identified by its black-tipped tail.

Bobcat

Bobcats are common on Point Reyes, but probably seen less often than foxes. They can be found in coastal canyons and along the edges of meadows.

The brush rabbit or cottontail is very common and can often be seen along the edges of trails passing through dense coyote bush. Their population is kept in check by foxes, bobcats, weasels, hawks and owls.

Brush Rabbit

Animal Tracks

Most animals are not easily seen. They are wary of open areas and many only appear at dusk or at night. Their footprints are the primary evidence we see during the daytime. The inside back cover shows footprints of some Point Reyes animals.

A10 Sea and Shore Birds

Common Goldeneye 18"
Bucephala clangula

Killdeer 10"
Charadrius vociferus

Willet 15"
Catoptrophorus semipalmatus

Bufflehead 14"
Bucephala albeola

Western Sandpiper 7"
Calidris mauri

Ruddy Duck 15"
Oxyura jamaicensis

American Oystercatcher 16"
Haematopus palliatus

Common Murre 16"
Uria aalge

Species	Spr	Sum	Fall	Wint	General Habitat
Common Goldeneye	2	5	2	2	Lagoons
Bufflehead	2	5	2	1	Lagoons - Ponds
Ruddy Duck	2	5	2	1	Lagoons
Killdeer	2	2	2	2	Grasslands - Ponds - Coastal
Amer. Oystercatcher	4	3	4	4	Coastal
Willet	2	5	1	1	Lagoons - Coastal
Western Sandpiper	1	5	1	1	Lagoons - Ponds
Common Murre	1	1	2	2	Coastal - Ocean
1 = Abundant, 2 = Common, 3 = Fairly Common, 4 = Uncommon, 5 = Rare					

Common Loon 32"
Gavia immer

Brandt's Cormorant 34"
*Phalaccrocorax
penicillatus*

Great Egret 39"
Casmerodius albus

Western Grebe 25"
*Aechmophorus
occidentalis*

Northern Pintail 27"
Anas acuta

Great Blue Heron 47"
Ardea herodias

Surf Scoter 19"
Melanitta perspicillata

Brown Pelican 50"
Pelecanus occidentalis

Species	Spr	Sum	Fall	Wint	General Habitat
Common Loon	3	5	3	1	Lagoons - Coastal
Western Grebe	3	5	3	2	Coastal - Lagoons
Brown Pelican	5	4	2	4	Lagoons - Coastal
Brandt's Cormorant	2	2	2	1	Coastal
Great Blue Heron	3	3	3	3	Lagoons
Great Egret	3	3	3	3	Lagoons
Northern Pintail	3	5	2	1	Lagoons - Ponds
Surf Scoter	2	4	3	1	Ocean - Lagoons - Coastal
1 = Abundant, 2 = Common, 3 = Fairly Common, 4 = Uncommon, 5 = Rare					

A11 Land Birds

Turkey Vulture 29"
Cathartes aura

Tree Swallow 5"
Tachycineta bicolor

Allen's Hummingbird 3"
Selasphorus sasin

Scrub Jay 12"
Aphelocoma coerulescens

Red-tailed Hawk 22"
Buteo jamaicensis

Acorn Woodpecker 9"
Melanerpes formicivorus

Pygmy Nuthatch 4"
Sitta pygmaea

California Quail 10"
Callipepla callifornica

Species	Spr	Sum	Fall	Wint	General Habitat
Turkey Vulture	2	2	2	2	Aerial
Red-tailed Hawk	2	2	2	2	Aerial - Scrub- Grasslands
California Quail	1	1	1	1	Scrub
Allen's Hummingbird	2	1	5	5	Streams - Scrub
Acorn Woodpecker	3	3	3	3	Forest - Visitor Center Area
Tree Swallow	2	3	3	5	Ponds - Forest
Scrub Jay	1	1	1	1	Scrub
Pygmy Nuthatch	3	3	3	3	Forest

1 = Abundant, 2 = Common, 3 = Fairly Common, 4 = Uncommon, 5 = Rare

Wrentit 6"
Chamaea fasciata

**Rufous-sided
Towhee 8"**
Pipilo erythrophthalmus

**Golden-crowned
Sparrow 6"**
Zonotrichia atricapilla

Hutton's Vireo 4"
Vireo huttoni

Tricolored Blackbird 8"
Agelaius tricolor

Wilson's Warbler 4"
Wilsonia pusilla

**White-crowned
Sparrow 6"**
Zonotrichia leucophrys

American Goldfinch 5"
Carduelis tristis

Species	Spr	Sum	Fall	Wint	General Habitat
Wrentit	2	2	2	2	Scrub
Hutton's Vireo	3	3	3	3	Forest - Streams
Wilson's Warbler	2	1	2	5	Streams - Forest
Rufous-sided Towhee	2	1	2	2	Scrub
White-crown Sparrow	2	2	1	1	Scrub
Golden-crown Sparrow	3	5	2	2	Scrub - Grasslands
Tricolored Blackbird	5	5	3	3	Pastures - Ponds
American Goldfinch	2	2	2	5	Grasslands - Scrub
1 = Abundant, 2 = Common, 3 = Fairly Common, 4 = Uncommon, 5 = Rare					

A12 Plant Communities

In his book, *The Natural History of Point Reyes*, Jules Evens states that, "Few areas on the North American landmass host the variety of habitats found within the 100 square miles on the Point Reyes Peninsula." The combination of latitude, climate, geology and topography have made Point Reyes a botanical treasure chest. When you visit Point Reyes, you'll discover four major plant communities, the Douglas fir forest, the Bishop pine forest, the coastal scrub and the grassland or pasture.

Douglas Fir Forest

The Douglas fir forest covers about 20% of the Point Reyes peninsula dominating the moister ridges, canyons and valleys. The Douglas fir is a majestic tree that can reach a height of 250' with a pyramid shaped crown. The one inch needles are splayed out at various angles and the 2-3 inch cones have a dozen or so small mouse-like tails that clearly distinguish them from other conifers.

Douglas Fir

Elderberry, huckleberry and ferns comprise most of the understory in the Douglas fir forest. You can get a good feel for the forest by hiking any of the trails out of Bear Valley and Five Brooks.

Bishop Pine Forest

Lying due north of the Douglas fir forest, on slightly drier slopes and canyons of Inverness Ridge, the Bishop pine forest covers about 13% of Point Reyes. Bishop pine grow from 40-60' in height and are similar in shape to Monterey pines. The needles of the Bishop pine are 2-4 inches long and come two to a bunch. (Monterey pines have slightly longer needles, three to a bunch.) The asymmetrical cones are tight swirls 3-5 inches in size that open to release seeds in hot weather or after fires.

Bishop Pine

Other plants found in the Bishop pine understory include coffeeberry, huckleberry, salal and in drier areas, manzanita and ceanothus.

A good way to practice distinguishing between Douglas fir and Bishop pine is to hike the transition zone between these communities which lies roughly between the Sky and Bayview trailhead. See Hike 17.

Coastal Scrub

The coastal scrub community covers about 15% of the peninsula with 4-6' shrubs that range from impenetrable thickets to isolated shrubs dotting grassy hillsides. The dominant plant is coyote bush, a nondescript shrub that forms white flowers in summer.

Joining the coyote bush in this community are sword fern, bracken fern, coffeeberry, bush lupine, monkeyflower, blackberry and poison oak. California sagebrush with grey-green needle-like leaves can also be found on drier slopes.

Coyote Bush

Grass, Prairie and Pasture

The largest area of Point Reyes, just over 50% is covered with grasses. Historically, much of this land has been used for dairy and cattle grazing and many of the native, perennial bunchgrasses have been replaced with non-native annuals like wild oats.

Other Communities

Several smaller areas on Point Reyes include the salt marsh, freshwater marsh, sand dune and riparian communities.

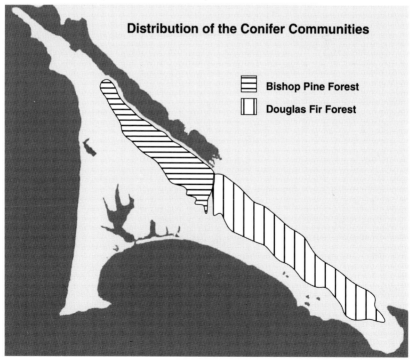

Distribution of the Conifer Communities

▤ **Bishop Pine Forest**

▥ **Douglas Fir Forest**

A13 Berries and Ferns

Two favorite groups of plants found on Point Reyes are berries and ferns. Ferns are treasured for their symmetry and delicate shape. Berries provide showy flowers and colorful fruit. All of the species shown below, except the blackberry, thrive in the shady canyons and ridges of the conifer forest where they are kept moist by winter rain and summer fog.

Berries

Berries grow on trees, shrubs, vines and groundcovers and come in a variety of flavors. Some are edible, some slightly toxic and some downright poisonous. An important Berry Rule is,

"Never taste a berry unless you know what it is."

Here are five of the most common berries found on Point Reyes and their suitablility for eating.

Red elderberry, to 15'
White flowers - spring
Red berries may be
toxic.

Thimbleberry, to 8'
White flowers - spring
Red berries in
summer are edible
when soft.

Huckleberry, to 10'
White flowers - spring
Blue berries in fall are
edible.

Red-Flowering
Currant, to 10'
Red flowers - early
spring. Purple berries
are barely edible.

Blackberry, vine to 5'
White flowers - spring
Blackberries range
from tart to sweet.

Ferns

Ferns are unusual in that the main part of the fern is a leaf, called a frond. More complex ferns, like the bracken fern, are a classic example of a fractal shape in nature. Fractals maintain similarity as you zoom in on them. Look closely at a bracken fern. The side leaflets are shaped just like the whole leaf. Likewise, the shape is repeated in the subleaflets.

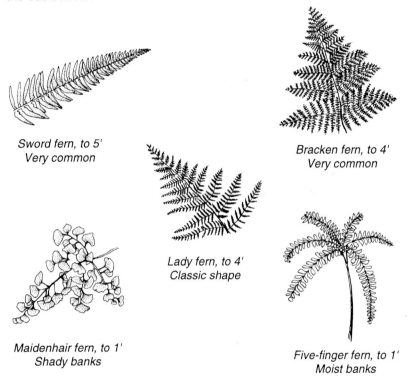

Sword fern, to 5'
Very common

Bracken fern, to 4'
Very common

Lady fern, to 4'
Classic shape

Maidenhair fern, to 1'
Shady banks

Five-finger fern, to 1'
Moist banks

Ferns are different from most plants in that they reproduce by spores rather than flowers and seeds. The life cycle of a fern includes two separate plants: a small, rarely-seen plant called a gametophyte and the sporophyte which we call a fern.

An individual fern can produce hundreds of thousands of spores in small capsules on the underside of each leaflet. After the capsule springs open, the spores are released and if conditions are right, grow into a gametophyte about 1/4" in size with male and female parts. If fertilization occurs, the fertilized egg develops into a new fern.

Hairy Star Tulip
Calochortus tolmiei
Plant height: 15 inches
Flower size: 1-2 inches
Leaf length: 5-12 inches
Season: April-July
Habitat: Moist, grassy coastal slopes

Milkmaids
Cardamine californica
Plant height: 16 inches
Flower size: 1/2 inch
Leaf length: 2 inches
Season: January-March
Habitat: Meadows, woods

Morning glory
Convolvulus occidentalis
Plant height: 4-6 feet
Flower size: 1-2 inches
Leaf length: 1 1/2 inches
Season: April-August
Habitat: Coastal scrub, rocky bluffs

Other common white - cream wildflowers are

Fairy Bells ..... Feb-Jul, 2 feet, white, bell-shaped flowers
Zigadene ..... Feb-Apr, 1-2 feet, white flower cluster
Alum-root ..... May-Jul, 2 feet, small white flowers
Yarrow ..... Apr-Sep, 18 inches, fern-like leaves, white flower cluster

Cow Parsnip
Heracleum lanatum
Plant height: 3-9 feet
Flower size: 1/2 -1 inch
Leaf length: 8-15 inches
Season: March-May
Habitat: Coastal scrub, grassland

Slim Solomon
Smilacina stellata var. sessilifolia
Plant height: 1-2 feet
Flower size: 1/4 inch
Leaf length: 2-6 inches
Season: February-April
Habitat: Wooded or brushy hills

Wild Cucumber
Marah fabaceous
Plant height: 10-20 feet
Flower size: 1/2 inch
Leaf length: 2-4 inches
Season: April-July
Habitat: Coastal dunes, coastal scrub

Wallflower
Erysimum concinnum
Plant height: 8-12 inches
Flower size: 1-1 1/2 inches
Leaf length: 1-3 inches
Season: February-July
Habitat: Coastal dunes, rocky bluffs

Buttercup
Ranunculus californicus
Plant height: 8-16 inches
Flower size: 1 inch
Leaf length: 1-1 1/2 inches
Season: February-May
Habitat: Low moist fields, brushy hills

California Poppy
Eschscholzia californica
Plant height: 8-16 inches
Flower size: 1-2 inches
Leaf length: 1-2 inches
Season: March-October
Habitat: Grassy hills, rocky slopes

Lizard Tail
Eriophyllum staechadifolium
Plant height: 1-5 feet
Flower size: 1/2 inch
Leaf length: 1-2 inches
Season: February-July
Habitat: Coastal scrub, coastal strand

Other common yellow - orange wildflowers are

Brass Buttons ..... Mar-Dec, 10 inches, yellow button-like flowers
Gumplant .....Jun-Aug, 1 foot, 2 inch daisy-like flowers
Sun Cups .....Feb-May, 4 inches, early flower, 4 yellow petals
Footsteps of Spring ..... Jan-May, 14 inches, early flower

Gold Fields
Lasthenia californica
Plant height: 8 inches
Flower size: 1 inch
Leaf length: 1/2 -1 inch
Season: March-June
Habitat: Meadows, grassy hills

Bush Monkeyflower
Mimulus aurantiacus
Plant height: 2-5 feet
Flower size: 1 1/2 -2 inches
Leaf length: 1-3 inches
Season: March-August
Habitat: Chaparral

Hairy Cat's Ear
Hypochoeris radicata
Plant height: 2-16 inches
Flower size: 1 inch
Leaf length: 3-6 inches
Season: April-December
Habitat: Widespread

Fiddleneck
Amsinckia intermedia
Plant height: 8 inches - 2 feet
Flower size: 1/2 inch
Leaf length: 1-6 inches
Season: March-June
Habitat: Grassland, ocean bluffs

Buckwheat
Eriogonum latifolium ssp. *nudum*
Plant height: 1-1 1/2 feet
Flower size: 1 inch
Leaf length: 1-2 inches
Season: June-November
Habitat: Rocky bluffs

Checkerbloom
Sidalcea malvaeflora
Plant height: 1-2 feet
Flower size: 1 inch
Leaf length: 1 inch
Season: March-May
Habitat: Open grassy hills

Farewell to Spring
Clarkia purpurea ssp. *quadrivulnera*
Plant height: 6-15 inches
Flower size: 1-1 1/2 inches
Leaf length: 1/2 -2 inches
Season: May-August
Habitat: Brushy or grassy slopes

Other common pink-red wildflowers are

Foxglove .....May-Aug, 3 feet, pink, hanging, bell-shaped flowers
Coyote Mint .....Jun-Sep, 1 foot, mint odor, pink flower heads
Sea Rocket .....May-Nov, 10 inches, succulent leaves, pink flowers
Johnny-tuck .....Mar-May, 6 inches, flower with white, pink and rose

Columbine
Aquilegia formosa
Plant height: 1-2 feet
Flower size: 1 inch
Leaf length: 2 inches
Season: April-June
Habitat: Brushy slopes, moist woods

Indian Paintbrush
Castilleja affinis
Plant height: 1-1 1/2 feet
Flower size: 1/2 -1 inch
Leaf length: 1-3 inches
Season: March-August
Habitat: Coastal scrub, coastal bluffs

Shooting Star
Dodecatheon hendersonii
Plant height: 8-16 inches
Flower size: 1 inch
Leaf length: 2-6 inches
Season: February-April
Habitat: Moist slopes

Sea Pink
Armeria maritima var. *californica*
Plant height: 1 1/2 -2 feet
Flower size: 1/2 inch
Leaf length: 2-6 inches
Season: April-August
Habitat: Coastal scrub, coastal bluffs

Blue Dicks
Brodiaea pulchella
Plant height: 1-2 feet
Flower size: 1 inch
Leaf length: 6-16 inches
Season: March-June
Habitat: Open or wooded hills

Blue-eyed Grass
Sisyrinchium bellum
Plant height: 6-18 inches
Flower size: 1/2 -1 inch
Leaf length: 4-24 inches
Season: March-May
Habitat: Open grassy hills

Douglas Iris
Iris douglasiana
Plant height: 6-18 inches
Flower size: 2-3 inches
Leaf length: 6-18 inches
Season: March-May
Habitat: Open grassy hills

Other common blue-purple wildflowers are

Baby Blue Eyes ..... Mar-May, 8 inches, pale-blue, one inch flowers
Sea Lavender ..... Jul-Dec, 18 inches, clusters of lavender flowers
Blue Coast Gilia ..... May-Jul, 1 foot, compact heads of blue flowers
California Phacelia ..... Apr-Jul, 1 foot, coil of lavender flowers

Hound's Tongue
Cynoglossum grande
Plant height: 1-3 feet
Flower size: 1/2 inch
Leaf length: 3-6 inches
Season: February-April
Habitat: Moist woods, brushy slopes

Hedge Nettle
Stachys rigida var. *quercetorum*
Plant height: 1-2 feet
Flower size: 1/2 -1 inch
Leaf length: 2-3 inches
Season: May-August
Habitat: Widespread

Bush Lupine
Lupinus arboreus
Plant height: 3-6 feet
Flower size: 1/2 inch
Leaf length: 1-2 inches
Season: March-August
Habitat: Coastal dunes, coastal scrub

Seaside Daisy
Erigeron glaucus
Plant height: 4-12 inches
Flower size: 1-1 1/2 inches
Leaf length: 4 inches
Season: May-August
Habitat: Coastal bluffs, coastal dunes

A18 Geology of Point Reyes

The theory of plate tectonics suggests that the earth's crustal surface, the upper forty miles, is composed of six major, rigid plates that move on a hot plastic interior. These plates are constantly interacting as new plate material oozes up in some areas, like Iceland, and old plate material disappears in other areas, like the deep sea trenches adjacent to the Aleutian Islands.

One of these plates, the Pacific plate containing Point Reyes, Los Angeles and most of the Pacific Ocean, is moving northwest relative to the North American plate and is slowly disappearing into the Alaskan trench. Although the Pacific plate is moving at an average speed of 1.3" per year, the motion is not steady. For example, where the two plates meet, as they do along the San Andreas and related fault lines, there can be sudden plate motion of up to 16 feet, as in the big San Francisco quake of 1906.

San Andreas Rift Zone

One of the most distinguishing features of the Point Reyes peninsula is the Olema Valley which runs northwesterly along Hwy. 1. This valley, including Tomales Bay, is prime evidence of the San Andreas rift zone, a collection of fault lines that mark the boundary of the North American and Pacific plates.

The Olema Valley offers a striking example of fault topography consisting of sag ponds, streams, small ridges and folded hills created by the uplifting, settling and shifting at the edges of these two great plates. Many of these features can be seen on the Earthquake, Olema Valley and Rift Zone trails.

The rocks to the east of the Olema Valley are a mixture of sandstone, greenstone, chert and serpentine that make up the Franciscan Formation. They are completely different from those of the Point Reyes peninsula which are mostly granite overlaid by marine deposits of sandstone, shale, siltstone, mudstone and greensand.

Granite

Granite is the underlying rock, the bedrock of the Point Reyes peninsula. However, two-thirds of this rock is now covered by layers of marine sediments. The exposed portion of the granite base lies mainly along the Inverness Ridge from Mt. Wittenberg north to Pierce Point. Examples of this mottled rock can be seen at the Visitor's Center and along the Earthquake, Sky and Tomales Point trails.

Marine Deposits

The largest of the marine layers is the Monterey Formation. It is composed of cherts and organic shales deposited and solidified in distinct layers of one to three inches thick. The Monterey Formation can be seen on the coastal cliffs from Duxbury Point to Bolinas Point. Outcroppings near Abbotts Lagoon and Kehoe Beach look like stepping stones, while roadside cuts near the Clem Miller Center appear as contorted slabs.

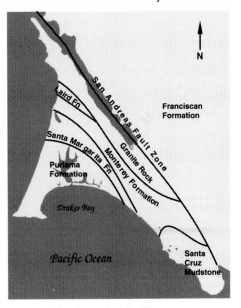

Geology of Point Reyes
Adapted from R. Melander, 1987
Clark, 1984 and Galloway, 1977

The next largest deposit, the Purisma Formation, consists of a softer sediment of muddy deposits. It is lightly colored and contains abundant microscopic fossils and occasional large fossils (collecting is prohibited). While it is not as widespread as the older Monterey shale, it is extensively exposed and easier to see, especially along Drakes Bay.

What is now called Santa Cruz Mudstone was originally thought to be part of the Monterey Formation. However, a fossil seacow discovered near Bolinas by College of Marin students indicated that the rocks were vastly different in age from the Monterey Formation. Subsequent work by the US Geological Survey clarified their origin.

The Pursima Formation and Santa Margarita Formation were thought to be unique to Point Reyes and were originally called the Drakes Bay Formation. Later, the USGS survey discovered that similar deposits existed elsewhere and the area was renamed.

It should be mentioned that topsoil ranging from one-half to three feet deep covers most of the formations mentioned here. These soils are formed by the mixing of the parent material with organic matter, a process that can produce unique soil and plant characteristics.

A19 Weather of Point Reyes

Point Reyes juts out into the Pacific Ocean, a geological, climatogical and vegetative island, riding the Pacific Plate on its northward journey relative to the mainland. Consequently, the weather on Point Reyes is dominated by the ocean. Summers at Point Reyes are cooler, and winters are warmer than areas inland. The difference in average temperature between summer and winter is just four degrees Fahrenheit. Although the temperature is fairly uniform, there are microclimates, significant climate differences that depend on location, terrain and season.

Winter

Winter at Point Reyes, from about mid-November to mid-March, is the rainy season. During this time, the jet stream often drops down over Northern California delivering a series of low pressure storm systems that dump an average of 10 to 60 inches of rain per year, depending on location. The headlands area gets the least rain. The lighthouse averages just 12 inches per year. Bear Valley averages 45 inches of rain per year.

Winter is not all storms, however. Between storms, some of the best coastal weather occurs. Often when much of northern California is socked in with cold, bone-chilling valley fog, Point Reyes basks in warm sunshine. This fog is produced by lack of winds and nighttime radiative cooling. At the coast, the moderating influence of the ocean keeps the temperature above the dew point and no fog develops, allowing the sun to warm Point Reyes from dawn to dusk.

Winter provides great hiking time, especially along the coast. Here, you find ocean waves crashing, grey whales migrating south, seals basking on the beaches, birds wintering in the marshes and lagoons, and in February, the first iris blooming on south-facing hills.

Spring

Spring is a time of transition. The weather is often unpredictable. Usually, by the middle of spring, northwest winds begin to establish a pattern which leads to either clear and windy, or foggy and windy, days. Occasionally, especially during El Nino years, the jet stream remains south keeping March and April wet and unsettled.

Some things are predictable in spring. Each April, the headlands, pasturelands and hills produce a glorious carpet of green, dotted with magnificent wildflowers. If the weather cooperates, spring can be the most exhilarating time to hike. It can also be a time to watch for returning whales and migrating birds.

Summer

Summer at Point Reyes, especially the headlands, can be cold, foggy windy and uncomfortable. The chaplain on Drake's expedition, Francis Fletcher, described it this way, "nipping colds as we have never seen before" and "thick mists and the most stinking fog". This was in June, 1579!

An interesting side note of the summer fog is that the entrance to San Francisco Bay was missed by European explorers for almost 200 years. It was not until 1769, that the Spanish explorer, Captain Gaspar de Portola, traveling by land, found this great natural harbor. Had the explorers sailed the coast in winter, they surely would have found the bay, but then they would have experienced the wrath of winter storms.

Why is the summer so inhospitable? The answer lies in the Pacific High, a high pressure system that forms off the California coast. This high produces northwest winds that create a surface current in the ocean that moves south. Because the earth rotates, any object that moves towards the equator, away from the axis of rotation, falls behind the earth's surface. In the northern hemisphere, south-moving objects like airplanes, winds and seas veer to the right. In the ocean, the south-moving surface current moves west, causing an upwelling of cold water along the coast. When warm, moisture-laden air gets close to the cold upwelled water, fog forms. On a typical summer day, this ocean fog will be sucked inland in the afternoon by hot air rising in the interior valleys. Later, the next day, the fog will burn off to the ocean. This cycle repeats itself with surprising regularity.

Fall

Like spring, fall is a period of transition. If the summer high stays in place, the winds and fog remain. However, once the Pacific High moves out of position, the upwelling ceases and Point Reyes experiences its warmest weather. Because the hills are dry and brown, the best way to enjoy this weather is to hike the coast, visit the beaches and explore tidepools.

Other changes also occur in fall. Willows, alders and buckeyes lose their leaves. Poison oak and blackberry shrubs provide red color and the big leaf maple turns yellow. Migrant and wintering birds begin to arrive and the first storms freshen the air.

A20 History of Point Reyes

Four hundred years ago, the population of the Point Reyes peninsula was greater than it is today! The late historian, Jack Mason, claimed that there were 113 village sites, mostly located around Tomales Bay, Drakes Estero and other seashore areas. These Native Americans were Coast Miwoks, described by Francis Fletcher, chaplain on Drake's expedition, as "a people of a tractable, free and loving nature, without guile or treachery."

The Miwoks had a rich variety of food at Point Reyes. They hunted small game, deer and elk, gathered acorns and berries and enjoyed the bounty of the sea – clams, mussels and fish. You can get some idea about how they lived by visiting Kule Loklo, a model village constructed in 1976 near park headquarters.

What happened to the Miwoks? The early 1800s were a disaster for them. Most of the Miwoks were persuaded to join the mission at San Rafael soon after it was established in 1817. Here, they took up agriculture and were to be baptized and civilized. The intentions of the missionaries may have been good, but the experiment failed. Disease, abuse and disenchantment with western ways set in. Shortly after secularization of the missions in 1934 by the Mexican government, a period of confrontation developed. When it was over in the late 1800s, the remaining Miwoks of Point Reyes scattered to the north.

Sir Francis Drake

Forty-one years before the landing of the Mayflower on Plymouth Rock, the English captain, Francis Drake, careened his sailing ship, the Golden Hind, on the soft sands at Drakes Estero. For 36 days, Drake worked to repair and replenish his ship before returning to England.

How do we know Drake landed at Point Reyes? Although there are an assortment of claims for other landing sites, such as Tomales Bay, Bolinas Lagoon, Bodega Bay and the Tiburon Peninsula,

Artists Conception of Drake Landing the Golden Hind

the overwhelming conclusion by historians here and in England is that Drake landed at Point Reyes. Their evidence includes:

- the description of the landing site as "white banks and cliffs", like those in England, which matches Drakes Bay better than anywhere else.
- the description of the weather as "nipping colds and stinking fogs" where they didn't see the sun or stars for 14 days.
- the reference to offshore islands which would be the Farallones.
- the map of New Albion made twelve years later by a Dutch cartographer that can be made to fit Drakes Estero.
- the description of meetings with local Native Americans.

A brass plate left behind by Drake and supposedly found near San Quentin in 1936 has been the subject of much controversy. It is now believed to be a prank.

Shipwrecks and the Coast Guard

The second European to set foot on Point Reyes suffered the ignoble site of seeing his ship wrecked at almost the exact spot of Drake's landing 16 years earlier. Sebastian Cermeno, sailing out of Acapulco, had arrived along the coast by way of Manila. His ship, the San Agustin, loaded with goods from the Orient, was battered and leaky after an arduous Pacific journey. In early November of 1595, a storm churned up southerly waves that ripped the San Agustin from its anchorage and drove her onto the beach where she was destroyed by pounding breakers.

Cermeno and 70 men set out in a small launch for Acapulco, leaving behind the San Agustin and its treasures. Three hundred and fifty years later, archeologists probing Miwok ruins in Drakes Bay, unearthed more than 100 fragments of Chinese porcelain identified as coming from the Wan Li period of the late 1500s. (Some historians argue that the porcelain actually came from the Drake expedition.)

The naval historian, Don Marshall, suggests that the Spaniard Cermeno found Drake's brass plate claiming New Albion for England and recorded the fact in his log. He reaches this conclusion by observing that Cermeno was a meticulus logkeeper, yet the entries surrounding his ships disappearance are almost non-existent. It seemed as though pages had been removed from the log.

Cermeno's shipwreck was the first of over fifty recorded shipwrecks along the Point Reyes peninsula. In 1841, the French trader Jose Yves Limantour, became stranded at what is now known as Limantour Spit. In 1861, a clippership sailed "fearlessly to her doom on Point Reyes beach with all sails set" according to Jack Mason.

By 1852, the large number of shipwrecks prompted Congress to appropriate $25,000 for a lighthouse. After 18 years of negotiation and construction, the lighthouse finally went into service 294 feet above sea level, yet 300 feet below the towering clifftop. Unfortunately, the light and its foghorn did not end shipwrecks. A Lifesaving Station was built in 1890 on Point Reyes Beach where it operated until 1927, when it was moved to Drakes Bay.

One of the most dramatic rescues took place in 1913 when the lumber schooner Samoa ran aground along the great beach. With spilled lumber thrashing in the surf, the lifesaving

The Wreck of the Somoa, 1913.

crew rigged a breeches buoy and safely removed everyone on board, one of the greatest breeches buoy rescues in U.S. history.

Dividing Up The Land

Between 1769 and 1823, Spain established 21 missions throughout California to solidify its presence and colonize the local population. When Mexico overthrew Spanish rule in 1822, they used the Mexican Land Grant to establish control. The great ranchos created by these grants were one of the most important influences in California history, as they concentrated land ownership in the hands of a select few.

During this time, Point Reyes was divided into two parcels: a 35,000 acre grant to John Berry, a colonel in the Mexican army and a 9,000 acre grant to Rafael Garcia, a corporal, once stationed at Yerba Buena. However, these grants contained vague conditions and overlapping boundaries, which left a heritage of confused land ownership. Speculators, sales, bad debts and land grabbers added to the confusion and when the dust settled in the late 1850s, Garcia and three gentlemen from Vermont owned most of the land. Their names,

Home Ranch, circa 1910

Oscar Shafter, James Shafter and Charles Howard would remain connected to Point Reyes up until World War II.

During the first half of the 20th century, Point Reyes was a rural area that supported cattle and dairy ranches, fishing and occasional hunters and vacationers. However, by the late 1950s, Point Reyes was on the verge of a major transition. A freeway was planned to connect Hwy. 101 to West Marin. A lumber mill was clearcutting Inverness Ridge. Developers were subdividing Limantour Beach and Lake Ranch. Hundreds of lots were available. Eighteen houses were built and sold. A marina and harbor were planned for Bolinas Lagoon. A large campground was planned on park land at Bear Valley. Shopping centers and new roads were being proposed to meet the new growth.

Creating a Park

Although there had been interest in creating a national park at Point Reyes as early as 1935, it was not until 1959 that Congress was persuaded to appropriate $15,000 to study the idea. Later that year, Congressman Clem Miller introduced legislation to acquire land.

This legislation intensified the political battle. How big would the park be? Developers continued to build, expecting that a park would increase land values. The ranchers were nervous and afraid of losing their land or their ability to sell their land for a profit. For three years, the debate raged. Congressman toured the area. Fortunately, the weather cooperated at key times and everyone agreed that Point Reyes was a special place worth saving.

Legislation creating the seashore was enacted and signed into law by President Kennedy in 1962. The park was to include 53,000 acres. A compromise was reached with the ranchers. It was agreed that 26,000 acres would remain the property of the current ranch owners. If they wanted to sell, the government would have the option to buy.

Although Congress voted to create a park, they didn't appropriate enough money to buy the land. By 1970, another crisis was brewing. It took a superhuman, grassroots effort by the Save Our Seashore committee to gather over 500,000 signatures and persuade Congress to appropriate sufficient funds to buy the remaining land.

The delay in completing the park had one unforeseen benefit. Originally, park planners hoped to make the park accessible for recreation, such as boating and camping. New and improved roads were planned. Later, in 1969, a new type of park was conceived. Much of the seashore was to be conserved as a wilderness. In 1976, 32,000 acres were designated the Philip Burton Wilderness Area, where no vehicles or man-made structures are allowed.

The early park conservationists have left us a wonderful legacy. Even though over two million people visit and use Point Reyes annually, it only takes a half-hour hike to get into the wilderness and enjoy the grandeur and solitude of this remarkable peninsula.

A21 Mt. Vision Fire of 1995

On Saturday, September 30, 1995, four teenagers made an illegal campfire on the top of Mt. Vision. The next day, they smothered the fire with dirt and left the campsite. However, they had not dug a fire pit down to bare earth, so smoldering embers remained. Two days later, on October 3, a strong, warm wind fanned the embers and started a major fire that burned for four days.

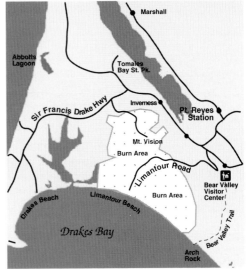
Extent of Fire

Over 2000 firefighters fought the blaze and by the time it was contained on October 7, it had covered 12,350 acres, destroyed 45 homes and damaged 10 others. All of the homes were on private property adjoining the National Park. For these people, the fire was a major tragedy. But what about the park. How did it survive?

Bishop Pine and Douglas Fir Forest

Of all the plant communities on Point Reyes, the Bishop Pine forest suffered the most damage. About half of the total Bishop pine on Point Reyes burned and died. However, in the long run, this is not bad news, but a necessary part of the Bishop pine life cycle.

Bishop Pine Forest

Bishop pine are a fire-adapted species. The cones of Bishop pine only open in intense heat. A few cones will open on a hot summer day, but after a fire, most cones open and scatter millions of seeds. These seeds propagate best when landing on ash and nutrient rich soil, clear of underbrush. The seeds germinate the following spring and the life cycle of the forest starts

122

again. Typically, Bishop pine need a fire every 30-80 years. If there is no fire, the trees become diseased and the forest may die out.

Shrubs in the understory of the Bishop pine forest, huckleberry, coffeeberry, ceanothus and manzanita are resprouters. After a fire, they send up shoots from the still-living base and recover quickly.

You can best see the effects of the fire on the Bishop pine forest by hiking from the Bayview Trailhead, Hikes 19 and 20.

The Douglas fir forest suffered much less than the Bishop pine forest. About 50% of the trees in the 500 acre burn area died, so that the visual effect is not as dramatic as in the Bishop pine forest. However,

*Bishop Pine Cone
Opened by the Fire*

firefighters created a firebreak by bulldozing the understory of the Douglas fir forest along Inverness Ridge, south of the Sky Trailhead. This ridgeline is practically a rain forest, so that evidence of the clearing will not last long. You can see the effects of the fire on the Douglas fir forest by hiking from the Sky Trailhead, Hikes 17 and 18.

Coastal Scrub and Grassland

Coastal scrub, consisting primarily of coyote bush with some coffeeberry, manzanita and ceanothus, are resprouters. After a fire, 30-80% of the burned plants will send up new growth from the base of the plant. You can see this best on Hike 20.

The coastal grassland recovered from the fires almost completely, even after one year. If you hike along the coast, Hike 21 or 22, you'll find it difficult to tell there was a fire.

Birds and Animals

Although there was a temporary loss of coastal scrub and reparian habitat for birds, the net effect of the fire was minimal. In fact, many species had a more successful fledgling rate because of fewer predators. For example, shrub nesters were successful producing fledglings 60% of the time compared with 30% in a control study.

Most large animals, deer, fox and bobcat escaped the fire and numbers have not changed much. The animal most affected by the fire was the Point Reyes mountain beaver, a small rodent that lives in burrows. In the burn area, almost 99% of the 2000 beavers died. This is about 60% of the total known population.

123

A22 Local Resources

Here is a partial list of the major lodging, food and other resources. Please call to verify hours and services. All numbers are in the 415 area code.

Point Reyes National Seashore
First-time visitors should stop at the main Visitor Center at Bear Valley to view exhibits and pick up information about a wide variety of ranger-led activities and hikes.
Bear Valley Visitor Center: 663-1092. Main Visitor Center.
Lighthouse Visitor Center: 669-1534. Check hours.
Drakes Beach Visitor Center: 669-1250. A cafe is located here.
Hostel information: 663-8811 early morning and evenings only.
Backpacking Reservations - call the Bear Valley Visitor Center.
Recorded Weather and Whale Information: 663-1092-x402

Point Reyes Station
Inns of Point Reyes - referral for several small inns: 663-1420
Seashore B&B's of Marin - referral service: 663-9373
West Marin Vacation Rentals - vacation homes: 1-800-540-1776
Point Reyes Lodging - inns and cottages: 663-1872
Station House Cafe: 663-1515
Point Reyes Roadhouse: 663-1277
Taqueria La Quinta: 663-8868
Joe's Family Diner: 663-1536
Bovine Bakery: 663-9420

Inverness and Inverness Park
Golden Hinde Inn and Marina - 35 rooms: 1-800-339-9398
Barnaby's By The Bay Restaurant: 669-1114
Inverness Valley Inn - 11 rooms: 669-7250
Inverness Motel - 7 rooms: 669-1081
Knave of Hearts Bakery: 663-1236
Grey Whale Pizza: 669-1244
Vladimiir's Restaurant: 669-1021
Manka's Czech Restaurant: 669-1034
Perry's Deli: 663-1491

Olema
Point Reyes Seashore Lodge - 18 rooms, 3 suites: 663-9000
Olema Farm House - Restaurant and Bar: 663-1264
Olema Ranch Campground - 32 acres - hookups: 1-800-655-2267
Olema Inn and Restaurant - 6 rooms: 663-9559

Bolinas
Bolinas Bay Bakery and Cafe: 868-0211
Blue Heron Inn and Restaurant - 2 rooms: 868-1102

Stinson Beach
Ocean Court Motel - 5 rooms: 868-0212
Sandpiper Motel - 5 rooms: 868-1632
Stinson Beach Motel - 6 rooms: 868-1712
Parkside Cafe: 868-1272
Sand Dollar Restaurant: 868-0434
Stinson Beach Grill: 868-2002

Rentals
Horses at Five Brooks Stables: 663-1570
Bicycles at Olema Trailhead Rental: 663-1958
Kayaks at Blue Waters Kayak - In Inverness: 669-2600
Kayaks at Tomales Bay Kayak - In Marshall: 663-1743

Education
Point Reyes Field Seminars: Call 663-1200 for a free schedule.
Point Reyes Bird Observatory: 868-1221

Gas Stations
Gas stations are located in Inverness, Point Reyes Station and the
campground at Olema. All are closed by 8 pm.

General Stores
General stores are located in Olema, Inverness, Inverness Park,
Point Reyes Station, Bolinas and Stinson Beach.

Oyster Companies
Johnson's Oyster Company - Sir Francis Drake Hwy: 669-1149
Hog Island Oyster Company - In Marshall on Hwy 1: 663-9218
Tomales Bay Oyster Company - Hwy 1: 663-1242

Campgrounds
In addition to those listed above, campgrounds are located at Pan
Toll, Mt. Tamalpais and Samuel P. Taylor State Parks.

Medical Services
West Marin Medical Center: 663-1082
Point Reyes Clinic: 663-8666

Emergency
Dial 911

A23 Bibliography

Arnot, Phil. *Point Reyes: Secret Places and Magic Moments.* Wide World Publishing, 1987.

Bakker, Elna. *An Island Called California.* University of California Press, 1971.

Beck, Warren A. and Haase, Ynez D. *Historical Atlas of California.* University of Oklahoma Press, 1974.

Burt, William and Grossenheider, Richard. *Mammals.* Peterson Field Guides, 1980.

Cobb, Boughton. *Ferns.* Peterson Field Guides, 1956.

Evens, Jules G. *The Natural History of the Point Reyes Peninsula.* Point Reyes National Seashore Association, 1988.

Gilliam, Harold. *Island in Time.* Sierra Club, 1962.

Gilliam, Harold. *Weather of the San Francisco Bay Region.* University of California Press, 1962.

Harrison, Tom. *Trail Map of Point Reyes National Seashore and Vicinity,* Tom Harrison Cartography, 1995

Hart, John. *Wilderness Next Door.* Presidio Press, 1979.

Jenkins, Olaf P., ed., *Geologic Guidebook of the San Francisco Bay Counties.* Department of Natural Resources, California, 1951.

Keator, Glenn and Heady, Ruth. *Pacific Coast Fern Finder.* Nature Study Guide, 1981.

Marshall, Don B. *California Shipwrecks.* Superior Publishing Company, 1978.

Mason, Jack. *Point Reyes: The Solemn Land.* North Shore Books, 1970.

Molenaar, Dee. *Point Reyes National Seashore: Pictorial Landform Map.* Wilderness Press, 1988.

Murie, Olaus. *A Field Guide to Animal Tracks.* Houghton Mifflin Company, 1954.

Parsons, Mary Elizabeth. *The Wild Flowers of California.* California Academy of Sciences, 1960.

Peterson, Roger Tory. *A Field Guide to Western Birds.* Houghton Mifflin Company, 1961.

Teather, Louise. *Place Names of Marin.* Scottwall Associates, 1986.

Von der Porten, Edward P. *Drake - Cermeno: An Analysis of Artifacts.* Drake Navigators Guild, 1965.

About the Authors

Kay Martin is the managing editor for scientific publications at the California Academy of Sciences. She also works as a volunteer docent for Bay Shore Studies and is active with the California Native Plant Society. In training for five marathons, she has logged several thousand miles running the trails of Marin County.

Don Martin has retired from the College of Marin where he taught physics and computer science. He has co-authored four computer books and has written and published a study guide. While Kay runs, Don jogs and occasionally rides his mountain bike.

The Martins have lived in San Anselmo since 1965. They are members of the Sierra Club, Tamalpa Runners, Audubon Society and St. Anselm's Church. They have four grown children. The Martins have also written and published the books, *MT TAM* and *Hiking Marin*.

Bob Johnson is a well-known Sonoma and Marin County illustrator. He has illustrated and designed dozens of books. In recent years, he has become very active in the wine industry, designing labels and packaging for many Sonoma and Napa wineries.

Books available from Martin Press:

Hiking Marin
121 Great Hikes in Marin County
Don and Kay Martin
© 1995
304 Pages, $18.95

MT TAM
A Hiking, Running and Nature Guide
Don and Kay Martin
2nd edition, © 1994
128 Pages, $9.95

Point Reyes National Seashore
A Hiking and Nature Guide
Don and Kay Martin
2nd edition, © 1997
136 Pages, $9.95

Many of the hikes in the two books, *Point Reyes National Seashore* and *MT TAM* also appear in the book, *Hiking Marin*. However, *Point Reyes National Seashore* and *MT TAM* include more detailed information about their respective areas.

All three books may be ordered from your local bookstore or directly from the publisher at the address below.

Please include $3.00 per book to cover shipping and tax.

Martin Press
P.O. Box 2109
San Anselmo, CA 94979